A CHRISTMAS STORY

Broadway Books
New York

A CHRISTMAS STORY

Jean Shepherd

PRINTED IN THE UNITED STATES OF AMERICA

Chapters 1 and 4 originally appeared in *Playboy*, Copyright 1964 and 1965 by HMH Publishing Co., Inc. Chapters 1, 2, 3, and 4 subsequently appeared in *In God We Trust, All Others Pay Cash* (Doubleday, 1966), Copyright 1966 by Jean Shepherd. Chapter 5 originally appeared in *Playboy*, Copyright 1966 by HMH Publishing Co., Inc. Chapter 5 subsequently appeared in *Wanda Hickey's Night of Golden Memories* (Doubleday, 1971), Copyright 1971 by Jean Shepherd.

Illustrated by George Peters Design & Illustration

ISBN-13: 978-0-7394-8998-7

The characters, places, and events described herein are entirely fictional, and any resemblance to individuals living or dead is purely coincidental, accidental, or the result of faulty imagination.

Jean Shepherd

CONTENTS

PUBLISHER'S NOTE

In 1983, a low-budget film titled *A Christmas Story* was released during the holiday season with little fanfare. Directed by Bob Clark, starring the wide-eyed Peter Billingsley as the young main character Ralphie Parker, and written for the screen by the cult humorist and radio monologist Jean Shepherd, it offered an affectionate but also slyly satirical portrait of a midwestern family's rites of Christmas during the Depression. It did modest business at the box office, but the second, televised life of *A Christmas Story* has proven nothing short of astonishing. Year by year, it has garnered more and more fans of its reality-based screwball comedy, so knowing about the ways of kids in an adult-controlled universe, until it now has become a cinematic holiday tradition to rival *It's a Wonderful Life* and *Miracle on 34th Street*. The film is ubiquitous on cable television in the week leading up to Christmas, and Ralphie Parker's dogged quest to have a Red Ryder BB Gun in the face of reported adult warnings that "You'll shoot your eye out" has entered the mass consciousness as an archetypal childhood experience. In a reconsideration of the film in his "Great Movies" series, famed film critic Roger Ebert writes that "there are many small but perfect moments in *A Christmas Story*" and that "some of the movie sequences stand as classic"—a verdict the film's millions of fans readily accept.

What has largely escaped notice in *A Christmas Story*'s rise to fame is that the film is drawn from a book by Jean Shepherd first published in 1966 (and never out of print since), *In God We Trust, All Others Pay Cash*. In writing his screenplay, Shepherd used material drawn from four of the fifteen autobiographical essays that comprise the book and wove it into the narrative of the film. This book version of *A Christmas Story* reprints those four pieces. The first and longest piece, "Duel in the Snow, *or* Red Ryder Nails the Cleveland Street Kid" recounts Ralphie Parker's quest for a BB gun for Christmas and various other incidents in the film. "The Counterfeit Secret Circle Member Gets the Message, *or* The Asp Strikes Again" deals with the Little Orphan Annie Decoder ring episode. "My Old Man and the Lascivious Special Award That Heralded the Birth of Pop Art" tells the story of the struggle between Ralph's father and mother over the leg-shaped lamp. And "Grover Dill and the Tasmanian Devil" is the almost epic narration of Ralph's victory over a local bully—here named Grover Dill but in the film called Scut Farkas. These essays together contain almost all of the anecdotes and the period and family details that make up the content and texture of the film.

The one exception is the climactic moment when the voracious hounds from the Bumpus family next door break into the Parker house and make off with the Christmas turkey. That incident is part of a longer essay about the Parkers' long-running feud with the Bumpuses, a terminally obnoxious family of hillbillies, titled "The Grandstand Passion Play of Delbert and the Bumpus Hounds." It is included here as a bonus selection—it is a ham, not a turkey, that disappears on Easter, not Christmas—taken from another Jean Shepherd collection, *Wanda Hickey's Night of Golden Memories*.

Jean Shepherd died in 1999, but his legacy as a master of humorous Americana endures, thanks to the film of *A Christmas Story*, his earlier books and now this new compilation. Readers who have enjoyed this book are urged to seek out Mr. Shepherd's other prose works—and, of course, to watch the film next Christmas.

DUEL IN THE SNOW, *OR* RED RYDER NAILS THE CLEVELAND STREET KID

DISARM THE TOY INDUSTRY

Printed in angry block red letters the slogan gleamed out from the large white button like a neon sign. I carefully reread it to make sure that I had not made a mistake.

DISARM THE TOY INDUSTRY

That's what it said. There was no question about it.

The button was worn by a tiny Indignant-type little old lady wearing what looked like an upturned flowerpot on her head and, I suspect (viewing it from this later date) a pair of Ked tennis shoes on her feet, which were primly hidden by the Automat table at which we both sat.

I, toying moodily with my chicken pot pie, which of

course is a specialty of the house, surreptitiously examined my fellow citizen and patron of the Automat. Wiry, lightly powdered, tough as spring steel, the old doll dug with Old Lady gusto into her meal. Succotash, baked beans, creamed corn, side order of Harvard beets. Bad news—a Vegetarian type. No doubt also a dedicated Cat Fancier.

Silently we shared our tiny Automat table as the great throng of pre-Christmas quick-lunchers eddied and surged in restless excitement all around us. Of course there were the usual H & H club members spotted here and there in the mob; out-of-work seal trainers, borderline bookies, ex-Opera divas, and panhandlers trying hard to look like Madison Avenue account men just getting out of the cold for a few minutes. It is an Art, the ability to nurse a single cup of coffee through an entire ten-hour day of sitting out of the biting cold of mid-December Manhattan.

And so we sat, wordlessly as is the New York custom, for long moments until I could not contain myself any longer.

"Disarm the Toy Industry?" I tried for openers.

She sat unmoved, her bright pink and ivory dental plates working over a mouthful of Harvard beets, attacking them with a venom usually associated with the larger carnivores. The red juice ran down over her powdered chin and stained her white lace bodice. I tried again:

"Pardon me, Madam, you're dripping."

"Eh?"

Her ice-blue eyes flickered angrily for a moment and

then glowed as a mother hen's looking upon a stunted, dwarfed offspring. Love shone forth.

"Thank you, sonny."

She dabbed at her chin with a paper napkin and I knew that contact had been made. Her uppers clattered momentarily and in an unmistakably friendly manner.

"Disarm the Toy Industry?" I asked.

"It's an outrage!" she barked, causing two elderly gentlemen at the next table to spill soup on their vests. Loud voices are not often heard in the cloistered confines of the H & H.

"It's an outrage the way the toymakers are forcing the implements of blasphemous War on the innocent children, the Pure in Spirit, the tiny babes who are helpless and know no better!"

Her voice at this point rising to an Evangelical quaver, ringing from change booth to coffee urn and back again. Four gnarled atheists three tables over automatically, by reflex action alone, hurled four "Amen's" into the unanswering air. She continued:

"It's all a Government plot to prepare the Innocent for evil, Godless War! I know what they're up to! Our Committee is on to them, and we intend to expose this decadent Capitalistic evil!"

She spoke in the ringing, anvil-like tones of a True Believer, her whole life obviously an unending fight against *They*, the plotters. She clawed through her enormous burlap handbag, worn paperback volumes of Dogma spilling out upon the floor as she rummaged frantically until she found what she was searching for.

"Here, sonny. Read this. You'll see what I mean." She handed me a smudgy pamphlet from some embattled group of Right Thinkers, based—of course—in California, denouncing the U.S. as a citadel of Warmongers, profit-greedy despoilers of the young and promoters of world-wide Capitalistic decadence, all through plastic popguns and Sears Roebuck fatigue suits for tots.

She stood hurriedly, scooping her dog-eared library back into her enormous rucksack and hurled her parting shot:

"Those who eat meat, the flesh of our fellow creatures, the innocent slaughtered lamb of the field, are doing the work of the Devil!"

Her gimlet eyes spitted the remains of my chicken pot pie with naked malevolence. She spun on her left Ked and strode militantly out into the crisp, brilliant Christmas air and back into the fray.

I sat rocking slightly in her wake for a few moments, stirring my lukewarm coffee meditatively, thinking over her angry, militant slogan.

DISARM THE TOY INDUSTRY

A single word floated into my mind's arena for just an instant—"Canal water!"—and then disappeared. I thought on: As if the Toy industry has any control over the insatiable desire of the human spawn to own Weaponry, armaments, and the implements of Warfare. It's the same kind of mind that thought if *making* whiskey were prohibited people would stop *drinking*.

I began to mull over my own youth, and, of course, its unceasing quest for roscoes, six-shooters, and any sort of blue hardware—simulated or otherwise—that I could lay my hands on. It is no coincidence that the Zip Green was invented by kids. The adolescent human carnivore is infinitely ingenious when confronted with a Peace movement.

Outside in the spanking December breeze a Salvation Army Santa Claus listlessly tolled his bell, huddled in a doorway to avoid the direct blast of the wind. I sipped my coffee and remembered another Christmas, in another time, in another place, and . . . a gun.

I remember clearly, itchingly, nervously, maddeningly the first time I laid eyes on it, pictured in a three-color, smeared illustration in a full-page back cover ad in *Open Road For Boys*, a publication which at the time had an iron grip on my aesthetic sensibilities, and the dime that I had to scratch up every month to stay with it. It was actually an early *Playboy*. It sold dreams, fantasies, incredible adventures, and a way of life. Its center foldouts consisted of gigantic Kodiak bears charging out of the page at the reader, to be gunned down in single hand-to-hand combat by the eleven-year-old Killers armed only with hunting knife and fantastic bravery.

Its Christmas issue weighed over seven pounds, its pages crammed with the effluvia of the Good Life of male Juvenalia, until the senses reeled and Avariciousness, the growing desire to own Everything, was almost unbearable. Today there must be millions of ex-subscribers who still can't pass Abercrombie & Fitch without a faint, keening note of desire and the unrequited urge to glom on to all of it. Just to have it, to feel it.

Early in the Fall the ad first appeared. It was a magnificent thing of balanced copy and pictures, superb artwork, and subtly contrived catch phrases. I was among the very first hooked, I freely admit it.

> *BOYS!* AT LAST *YOU* CAN OWN AN *OFFICIAL RED RYDER* CARBINE ACTION TWO-HUNDRED-SHOT *RANGE MODEL AIR RIFLE!*

This in block red and black letters surrounded by a large balloon coming out of Red Ryder's own mouth, wearing his enormous ten-gallon Stetson, his jaw squared, staring out at me manfully and speaking directly to me, eye to eye. In his hand was the knurled stock of as beautiful, as coolly deadly-looking a piece of weaponry as I'd ever laid eyes on.

> YES, FELLOWS. . . .

Red Ryder continued under the gun:

> YES, FELLOWS, THIS TWO-HUNDRED-SHOT CARBINE ACTION AIR RIFLE, JUST LIKE THE ONE I USE IN ALL

MY RANGE WARS CHASIN' THEM RUSTLERS AND BAD GUYS CAN BE YOUR VERY OWN! IT HAS A SPECIAL BUILT-IN SECRET COMPASS IN THE STOCK FOR TELLING THE DIRECTION IF YOU'RE LOST ON THE TRAIL, AND ALSO AN OFFICIAL RED RYDER SUNDIAL FOR TELLING TIME OUT IN THE WILDS. YOU JUST LAY YOUR CHEEK 'GAINST THIS STOCK, SIGHT OVER MY OWN SPECIAL DESIGN CLOVERLEAF SIGHT, AND YOU JUST CAN'T MISS. TELL DAD IT'S GREAT FOR TARGET SHOOTING AND VARMINTS, AND IT WILL MAKE A SWELL CHRISTMAS GIFT!!

The next issue arrived and Red Ryder was even more insistent, now implying that the supply of Red Ryder BB guns was limited and to order now or See Your Dealer Before It's Too Late!

It was the second ad that actually did the trick on me. It was late November and the Christmas fever was well upon me. I thought about a Red Ryder air rifle in all my waking hours, seven days a week, in school and out. I drew pictures of it in my Reader, in my Arithmetic book, on my hand in indelible ink, on Helen Weathers' dress in front of me, in crayon. For the first time in my life the initial symptoms of genuine lunacy, of Mania, set in.

I imagined innumerable situations calling for the instant and irrevocable need for a BB gun, great fantasies where I fended off creeping marauders burrowing through the snow toward the kitchen, where only I and I alone stood between our tiny huddled family and insensate Evil. Masked bandits attacking my father, to be mowed down by my trusted cloverleaf-sighted deadly weapon. I seriously mulled over the possibility of an invasion of raccoons, of which there were several in the county. Acts of selfless Chivalry defending Esther Jane Alberry from escaped circus tigers. Time and time again I saw myself a miraculous crack shot, picking off sparrows on the wing to the gasps of admiring girls and envious rivals on Cleveland Street. There was one dream that involved my entire class getting lost on a field trip in the swamps, wherein I led the tired, hungry band back to civilization, using only my Red Ryder compass and sundial. There was no question about it. Not only should I have such a gun, it was an absolute *necessity*!

Early December saw the first of the great blizzards of that year. The wind howling down out of the Canadian wilds a few hundred miles to the north had screamed over frozen Lake Michigan and hit Hohman, laying on the town great drifts of snow and long, story-high icicles, and subzero temperatures where the air cracked and sang. Streetcar wires creaked under caked ice and kids plodded to school through forty-five-mile-an-hour gales, tilting forward like tiny furred radiator ornaments, moving stiffly over the barren, clattering ground.

Preparing to go to school was about like getting ready for extended Deep-Sea Diving. Longjohns, corduroy knickers, checkered flannel Lumberjack shirt, four sweaters, fleece-lined leatherette sheepskin coat, helmet, goggles, mittens with leatherette gauntlets and a large red star with an Indian Chief's face in the middle, three pair of sox, high-tops, overshoes, and a sixteen-foot scarf wound spirally from left to right until only the faint glint of two eyes peering out of a mound of moving clothing told you that a kid was in the neighborhood.

There was no question of staying home. It never entered anyone's mind. It was a hardier time, and Miss Bodkin was a hardier teacher than the present breed. Cold was something that was accepted, like air, clouds, and parents; a fact of Nature, and as such could not be used in any fraudulent scheme to stay out of school.

My mother would simply throw her shoulder against the front door, pushing back the advancing drifts and stone ice, the wind raking the living-room rug with angry fury for an instant, and we would be launched, one after the other, my brother and I, like astronauts into unfriendly Arctic space. The door clanged shut behind us and that was it. It was make school or die!

Scattered out over the icy waste around us could be seen other tiny befurred jots of wind-driven humanity. All painfully toiling toward the Warren G. Harding School, miles away over the tundra, waddling under the weight of frost-covered clothing like tiny frozen bowling balls with feet. An occasional piteous whimper would be heard faintly, but lost instantly in the sigh of the eternal wind. All of us were bound for geography lessons involving the exports of Peru, reading lessons dealing with fat cats and dogs named

Jack. But over it all like a faint, thin, offstage chorus was the building excitement. Christmas was on its way. Each day was more exciting than the last, because Christmas was one day closer. Lovely, beautiful, glorious Christmas, around which the entire year revolved.

Off on the far horizon, beyond the railroad yards and the great refinery tanks, lay our own private mountain range. Dark and mysterious, cold and uninhabited, outlined against the steel-gray skies of Indiana winter, the Mills. It was the Depression, and the natives had been idle so long that they no longer even considered themselves out of work. Work had ceased to exist, so how could you be out of it? A few here and there picked up a day or so a month at the Roundhouse or the Freight yards or the slag heaps at the Mill, but mostly they just spent their time clipping out coupons from the back pages of *True Romances* magazine, coupons that promised virgin territories for distributing ready-made suits door to door or offering untold riches repairing radios through correspondence courses.

Downtown Hohman was prepared for its yearly bacchanalia of peace on earth and good will to men. Across Hohman Avenue and State Street, the gloomy main thoroughfares—drifted with snow that had lain for months and would remain until well into Spring, ice encrusted, frozen drifts along the curbs—were strung strands of green and red Christmas bulbs, and banners that snapped and cracked in the gale. From the streetlights hung plastic ivy wreaths surrounding three-dimensional Santa Claus faces.

For several days the windows of Goldblatt's department store had been curtained and dark. Their corner window was traditionally a major high-water mark of the pre-Christmas season. It set the tone, the motif of their giant Yuletide Jubilee. Kids were brought in from miles around just to see the window. Old codgers would recall vintage years when the window had flowered more fulsomely than in ordinary times. This was one of those years. The magnificent display was officially unveiled on a crowded Saturday night. It was an instant smash hit. First Nighters packed earmuff to earmuff, their steamy breath clouding up the sparkling plate glass, jostled in rapt admiration before a golden, tinkling panoply of mechanized, electronic Joy.

This was the heyday of the Seven Dwarfs and their virginal den mother, Snow White. Walt Disney's seven cutiepies hammered and sawed, chiseled and painted while Santa, bouncing Snow White on his mechanical knee, ho-ho-ho'd through eight strategically placed loudspeakers—interspersed by choruses of "Heigh ho, heigh ho, it's off to work we go." Grumpy sat at the controls of a miniature eight-wheel Rock Island Road steam engine and Sleepy played a marimba, while in the background, inexplicably, Mrs. Claus ceaselessly ironed a red shirt. Sparkling artificial snow drifted down on Shirley Temple dolls, Flexible Flyers, and Tinker Toy sets glowing in the golden spotlight. In the foreground a frontier stockade built of Lincoln Logs was manned by a company of kilted lead Highlanders who were doughtily fending off an attack by six U.S. Army medium tanks. (History has always been vague in Indiana.) A few feet away stood an Arthurian cardboard castle with Raggedy Andy sitting on the drawbridge, his feet in the moat, through which a Lionel freight train burping real smoke went round and round. Dopey sat in Amos and Andy's pedal-operated Fresh Air Taxicab beside a stuffed panda holding a lollipop in his paw, bearing the heart-tugging legend, "Hug me." From fluffy cotton clouds above, Dionne quintuplet dolls wearing plaid golf knickers hung from billowing parachutes, having just bailed out of a high-flying balsawood Fokker triplane. All in all, Santa's workshop made Salvador Dali look like Norman Rockwell. It was a good year. Maybe even a great one. Like a swelling Christmas balloon, the excitement mounted until the whole town tossed restlessly in bed—and made plans for the big day. Already my own scheme was well under way, my personal dream. Casually, carefully, calculatingly, I had booby-trapped the house with copies of *Open Road For Boys*, all opened to Red Ryder's slit-eyed face. My father, a great john reader, found himself for the first time in his life in alien literary waters. My mother, grabbing for her copy of *Screen Romances*, found herself cleverly euchred into reading a Red Ryder sales pitch; I had stuck a copy of *ORFB* inside the cover showing Clark Gable clasping Loretta Young to his heaving breast.

At breakfast I hinted that there was a rumor of loose bears in the neighborhood, and that I was ready to deal with them if I had the proper equipment. At first my mother and the Old Man did not rise to the bait, and I began to push, grow anxious, and, of course, inevitably overplayed my hand. Christmas was only weeks away, and I could not waste time with subtlety or droll innuendo.

My brother, occasionally emerging from under the daybed during this critical period, was already well involved in some private Little Brother persiflage of his own involving an Erector Set with motor, capable of constructing drawbridges, Eiffel towers, Ferris wheels, and operating guillotines. I knew that if he got wind of *my* scheme, all was lost. He would then begin wheedling and whining for what I wanted, which would result in nobody scoring, since he was obviously too young for deadly weapons. So I cleverly pretended that I wanted nothing more than a simple, utilitarian, unpretentious Sandy Andy, a highly symbolic educational toy popular at the time, consisting of a kind of funnel under which was mounted a tiny conveyor belt of little scooplike gondolas. It came equipped with a bag of white sand that was poured into the funnel. The sand trickling out of the bottom into the gondolas set the belt in motion. As each gondola was filled, it moved down the track to be replaced by another, which, when filled, moved down another notch. And endlessly they went, dumping sand out at the bottom of the track and starting up the back loop to be refilled again—on and on until all the sand was deposited in the red cup at the bottom of the track. The kid then emptied the cup into the funnel and it started all over again—ceaselessly, senselessly, round and round. How like Life itself; it was the perfect toy for the Depression. Other kids in the neighborhood were embarked on grandiose, pie-in-the-sky dreams of Lionel electric trains, gigantic Gilbert chemistry sets, and other totally unimaginable impossibilities.

Through my brain nightly danced visions of six-guns snapped from the hip and shattering bottles—and a gnawing nameless frenzy of impending ecstasy. Then came my first disastrous mistake. In a moment of unguarded rashness I brought the whole plot out into the open. I was caught by surprise while pulling on my high-tops in the kitchen, huddled next to the stove, the only source of heat in the house at that hour of the morning. My mother, leaning over a pot of simmering oatmeal, suddenly asked out of the blue:

"What would you like for Christmas?"

Horrified, I heard myself blurt: "A Red Ryder BB gun!"

Without pausing or even missing a stroke with her tablespoon, she shot back: "Oh no. You'll shoot out one of your eyes."

It was the classic Mother BB Gun Block! I was sunk! That deadly phrase, used many times before by hundreds of mothers, was not surmountable by any means known to Kid-dom. I had really booted it, but such was my mania, my desire for a Red Ryder carbine, that I immediately began to rebuild the dike.

"I was just kidding. Even though Flick is getting one. (A lie.) I guess . . . I guess . . . I sure would like a Sandy Andy, I guess."

I watched the back of her Chinese red chenille bathrobe

anxiously, looking for any sign that my shaft had struck home.

"They're dangerous. I don't want anybody shooting their eyes out."

The boom had been lowered and I was under it. With leaden heart and frozen feet I waddled to school, bereft but undaunted.

At Recess time little knots of kids huddled together for warmth amid the gray craggy snowbanks and the howling gale. The telephone wires overhead whistled like banshees while the trapeze rings on the swings clanked hollowly as Schwartz and Flick and Bruner and I discussed the most important thing next to What I'm Going To Get For Christmas, which was What I'm Getting My Mother and Father For Christmas. We talked in hushed, hoarse whispers to guard against Security leaks. The selection of a present was always done with greater secrecy than that which usually surrounds a State Department White Paper on Underground Subversive Operations in a Foreign Country. Schwartz, his eyes darting over his shoulder as he spoke, leaned into the wind and hissed:

"I'm getting my father. . . ."

He paused dramatically, hunching forward to exclude unfriendly ears, his voice dropping even lower. We listened intently for his punchline.

". . . a new Flit gun!"

The sheer creative brilliance of it staggered us for a moment. Schwartz smiled smugly, his earmuffs bobbing jauntily as he leaned back into the wind, knowing he had scored. Flick, looking suspiciously at a passing female first grader who could be a spy for his mother, waited until the coast was clear and then launched his entry into the icy air.

"For my father I'm getting. . . ."

Again we waited, Schwartz with a superior smirk playing faintly on his chapped lips.

". . . a rose that *squirts!*"

We had all seen these magnificent appliances at George's Candy Store, and instantly we saw that this was a gift *anyone* would want. They were bright-red celluloid, with a white rubber bulb for pocket use. At this point, luckily, the bell rang, calling us back to our labors before I had to divulge my own gifts, which I knew did not come up to these magnificent strokes of genius.

I had not yet made an irrevocable choice for my mother, but I had narrowed the field down to two spectacular items I had been stealthily eying at Woolworth's for several weeks. The first was a tasteful string of beads about the size of small walnuts, brilliant ruby in color with tiny yellow flowers embedded in the glass. The other and more expensive gift—$1.98—was a pearl-colored perfume atomizer, urn-shaped, with golden lion's feet and matching gold top and squeeze bulb. It was not an easy choice. It was the age-old conflict between the Classic and the Sybaritic, and that is never easily resolved.

For my father, I had already made the down payment on a family-size can of Simoniz. One of my father's favorite proverbs, one he never tired of quoting, was:

"Motorists wise, Simoniz."

He was as dedicated a hood-shiner as ever bought a fourth-hand Graham-Paige, with soaring hopes and bad valves. I could hardly wait to see him unwrap the Simoniz on Christmas Eve, with the light of the red, yellow, green, and blue bulbs on the tree making that magnificent can glow like the deep flush of myrrh and frankincense. It was all I could do, a constant tortured battle, to keep myself from spilling the beans and thus destroying the magnificent moment of stunned surprise, the disbelieving delight which I knew would fell him like a thunderclap when he saw that I had gone all out.

In fact, several times over the supper table I had meaningfully asked:

"I'll bet you can't guess what I got you for Christmas, Dad."

Once, instead of saying: "Hmmmmm," he answered by saying: "Hmmm. Let's see. Is it a new furnace?"

My kid brother fell over sideways in nutty little-kid laughter and knocked over his milk, because my father was one of the most feared Furnace Fighters in Northern Indiana.

"That clanky old son of a bitch," he called it, and many's the night with the snow drifting in through the Venetian blinds and the windows rattling like frozen tom-toms he would roar down the basement steps, knocking over Ball jars and kicking roller skates out of the way, bellowing:

"THAT SON OF A BITCH HAS GONE OUT AGAIN! THAT GODDAMN CLANKY SON OF A BITCH!!"

The hot-air registers breathed into the clammy air the whistling breath of the Antarctic. A moment of silence. The stillness of the tundra gripped the living room; the hoarfrost sparkled like jewels in the moonlight on my mother's Brillo pad in the kitchen sink.

CLANK! K-BOOM! CLANK! K-BOOM! *CLANK!*

"SONOFABITCH!"

CLANK! K-BOOM! K-BOOM! CLANKCLANK!

He would be operating something called The Shaker, a long iron handle that stuck out of the bottom of that zinc and tin monster called The Furnace.

"For Chrissake, open up the goddamn damper, willya! How the hell did it get turned all the way down again!? GODDAMMIT!"

My mother would leap out of bed and rush into the kitchen in the dark to pull a chain behind the broom closet door marked "Draft."

"FOR CHRISSAKE, STUPID, I SAID THE GODDAMN *DAMPER!*"

My kid brother and I would huddle under our baseball quilt in our Dr. Denton Sleepers, waiting for the uproar to strike us. That's why my brother knocked over the milk when my Old Man said the thing about a new furnace. Indiana wit is always pungent and to the point.

My father was also an expert Clinker Fisher. The furnace was always producing something called "clinkers" which got stuck in the grates, causing faint puffs of blue smoke to come out from under the daybed.

"Sonofabitch clinker!"

The Old Man would jump up at the first whiff and rush down into the basement for a happy night at the old iron fishing hole with his trusty poker. People in Northern Indiana fought Winter tooth and claw; bodily, and there was never a letup.

I had not yet decided on what to get my kid brother for Christmas. It was going to be either a rubber dagger or a Dick Tracy Junior Crimefighter Disguise Kit, containing three false noses and a book of instructions on how to trap crooks. Picking something for your kid brother is never easy, particularly if what you get him is something you yourself have always wanted. This can lead to nothing but bad blood, smoldering rivalries, and scuffling in the bathroom. I myself was lukewarm on rubber daggers at this point in the game, so I was inclined to figure that a good big one with a painted silver blade might do the trick. I was a little doubtful about the Dick Tracy Kit, since I sensed vaguely that there might be trouble over one of the noses, a large orange job with plastic horn-rimmed glasses attached. A dark-horse possibility was a tin zeppelin with red propellers and blue fins. I figured this was something you could really get your teeth into, and it was what I eventually decided on, not realizing that one of the hardest things to wrap in green tissue paper with Santa Claus stickers and red string is a silver zeppelin. Zeppelins are not easy to disguise.

It was now the second week of December and all the stores in town stayed open nights, which meant that things were really getting serious. Every evening immediately after supper we would pile into the car and drive downtown for that great annual folk rite, that most ecstatic, golden, tinseled, quivering time of all kidhood: Christmas shopping. Milling crowds of blue-jowled, agate-eyed foundry workers, gray-faced refinery men, and motley hordes of open-hearth, slag-heap, Bessemer-converter, tin-mill, coke-plant, and welding-shop fugitives trudged through the wildly pulsing department stores, through floor after floor of shiny, beautiful, unattainable treasures, trailed by millions of leatherette-jacketed, high-topped, mufflered kids, each with a gnawing hunger to Get It All. Worried-looking, flush-faced mothers wearing frayed cloth coats with ratty fox-fur collars, their hands chapped and raw from years of dish-water therapy, rode herd on the surging mob, ranging far and wide into the aisles and under the counters, cuffing, slapping, dragging whiners of all sizes from department to department.

At the far end of Toyland in Goldblatt's, on a snowy throne framed with red-and-white candy canes under a suspended squadron of plastic angels blowing silver trumpets in a glowing golden grotto, sat the Man, the Connection: Santa Claus himself. In Northern Indiana Santa Claus is a *big* man, both spiritually and physically, and the Santa Claus at Goldblatt's was officially recognized among the kids as being unquestionably THE Santa Claus. In person. Eight feet tall, shiny high black patent-leather boots, a nimbus cloud of snow-white beard, and a real, thrumming, belt-creaking stomach. No pillows or stuffing. I mean a real *stomach!*

A long line of nervous, fidgeting, greedy urchins wound in and out of the aisles, shoving, sniffling, and above all waiting, waiting to tell HIM what they wanted. In those days it was not easy to disbelieve fully in Santa Claus, because there wasn't much else to believe *in*, and there were many theological arguments over the nature of, the existence of, the affirmation and denial of his existence. However, ten days before zero hour, the air pulsing to the strains of "We Three Kings of Orient Are," the store windows garlanded with green-and-red wreaths, and the toy department bristling with shiny Flexible Flyers, there were few who *dared* to disbelieve. As each day crept on to the next like some arthritic glacier, the atheists among us grew moodier and less and less sure of ourselves, until finally in each scoffing heart was the floating, drifting, nagging suspicion:

"Well, you never can tell."

It did not pay to take chances, and so we waited in line for our turn. Behind me a skinny seven-year-old girl wearing a brown stocking cap and gold-rimmed glasses hit her little brother steadily to keep him in line. She had green teeth. He was wearing an aviator's helmet with the goggles pulled down over his eyes. His galoshes were open and his maroon corduroy knickers were damp. Behind them a fat boy in a huge sheepskin coat stood numbly, his eyes watering in vague fear, his nose red and running. Ahead of my brother and me, a long, uneven procession of stocking caps, mufflers, mittens, and earmuffs inched painfully forward, while in the hazy distance, in his magic glowing cave, Mister Claus sat each in turn on his broad red knee and listened to exultant dream after exultant dream whispered, squeaked, shouted, or sobbed into his shell-like, whisker-encased ear.

Closer and closer we crept. My mother and father had stashed us in line and disappeared. We were alone. Nothing stood between us and our confessor, our benefactor, our patron saint, our dispenser of BB guns, but 297 other beseechers at the throne. I have always felt that later generations of tots, products of less romantic upbringing, cynical nonbelievers in Santa Claus from birth, can never know the nature of the true dream. I was well into my twenties before I finally gave up on the Easter bunny, and I am not convinced that I am the richer for it. Even now there are times when I'm not so sure about the stork.

Over the serpentine line roared a great sea of sound: tinkling bells, recorded carols, the hum and clatter of electric trains, whistles tooting, mechanical cows mooing, cash registers dinging, and from far off in the faint distance the "Ho-ho-ho-ing" of jolly old Saint Nick.

One moment my brother and I were safely back in the Tricycle and Irish Mail department and the next instant we stood at the foot of Mount Olympus itself. Santa's enormous gleaming white snowdrift of a throne soared ten or fifteen feet above our heads on a mountain of red and green tinsel carpeted with flashing Christmas-tree bulbs and gleaming ornaments. Each kid in turn was prodded up a tiny staircase at the side of the mountain on Santa's left, as he passed his last customer on to his right and down a red chute—back into oblivion for another year.

Pretty ladies dressed in Snow White costumes, gauzy gowns glittering with sequins, and tiaras clipped to their golden, artificial hair, presided at the head of the line, directing traffic and keeping order. As we drew nearer, Santa seemed to loom larger and larger. The tension mounted. My brother was now whimpering steadily. I herded him ahead of me while, behind, the girl in the glasses did the same with *her* kid brother. Suddenly there was no one left ahead of us in the line. Snow White grabbed my brother's shoulder with an iron grip and he was on his way up the slope.

"Quit dragging your feet. Get moving," she barked at the toiling little figure climbing the stairs.

The music from above was deafening:

JINGLE BELLS, JINGLE BELLS, JINGLE ALL THE WAY. . . .

sung by 10,000 echo-chambered, reverberating chipmunks. . . .

High above me in the sparkling gloom I could see my brother's yellow-and-brown stocking cap as he squatted briefly on Santa's gigantic knee. I heard a booming "Ho-ho-ho," then a high, thin, familiar, trailing wail, one that I had heard billions of times before, as my brother broke into his Primal cry. A claw dug into my elbow and I was launched upward toward the mountaintop.

I had long before decided to level with Santa, to really lay it on the line. No Sandy Andy, no kid stuff. If I was going to ride the range with Red Ryder, Santa Claus was going to have to get the straight poop.

"AND WHAT'S YOUR NAME, LITTLE BOY?"

His booming baritone crashed out over the chipmunks. He reached down and neatly hooked my sheepskin collar, swooping me upward, and there I sat on the biggest knee in creation, looking down and out over the endless expanse of Toyland and down to the tiny figures that wound off into the distance.

"Uhh . . . uhhh . . . uhhh. . . ."

"THAT'S A FINE NAME, LITTLE BOY! HO-HO-HO!"

Santa's warm, moist breath poured down over me as though from some cosmic steam radiator. Santa smoked Camels, like my Uncle Charles.

My mind had gone blank! Frantically I tried to remember what it was I wanted. I was blowing it! There was no one else in the world except me and Santa now. And the chipmunks.

"Uhhh . . . ahhhh. . . ."

"WOULDN'T YOU LIKE A NICE FOOTBALL?"

My mind groped. Football, football. Without conscious will, my voice squeaked out:

"Yeah."

My God, a football! My mind slammed into gear. Already Santa was sliding me off his knee and toward the red chute, and I could see behind me another white-faced kid bobbing upward.

"*I want a Red Ryder BB gun with a special Red Ryder sight and a compass in the stock with a sundial!*" I shouted.

"HO-HO-HO! *YOU'LL SHOOT YOUR EYE OUT, KID.* HO-HO-HO! MERRY CHRISTMAS!"

Down the chute I went.

I have never been struck by a bolt of lightning, but I know how it must feel. The back of my head was numb. My feet clanked leadenly beneath me as I returned to earth at the bottom of the chute. Another Snow White shoved the famous free gift into my mitten—a barely recognizable plastic Kris Kringle stamped with bold red letters: MERRY XMAS. SHOP AT GOLDBLATT'S FREE PARKING—and spun me back out into Toyland. My brother stood sniveling under a counter piled high with Raggedy Ann dolls, from nowhere my mother and father appeared.

"Did you tell Santa what you wanted?" the Old Man asked.

"Yeah. . . ."

"Did he ask you if you had been a good boy?"

"No."

"Ha! Don't worry. He knows anyway. I'll bet he knows about the basement window. Don't worry. He knows."

Maybe *that* was it! My mind reeled with the realization that maybe Santa *did* know how rotten I had been and that the football was not only a threat but a punishment. There had been for generations on Cleveland Street a theory that if you were not "a good boy" you would reap your just desserts under the Christmas tree. This idea had been largely discounted by the more confirmed evildoers in the neighborhood, but now I could not escape the distinct possibility that there was something to it. Usually for a full month or so before the big day most kids walked the straight and narrow, but I had made a drastic slip from the paths of righteousness by knocking out a basement window with a sled runner and then compounding the idiocy by denying it when all the evidence was incontrovertible. This caused an uproar which had finally resulted in my getting my mouth washed out with Lux and a drastic curtailment of allowance to pay for the glass. I could see that either my father or Santa, or perhaps both, were not content to let bygones be bygones. Were they in league with each other? Or was Santa actually a mother in disguise?

The next few days groaned by. Now only three more school days remained before Christmas vacation, that greatest time of all the year. As it drew closer, Miss Iona Pearl Bodkin, my homeroom teacher, became more and more manic, whipping the class into a veritable frenzy of Yuletide joy. We belted out carol after carol. We built our own paper Christmas tree with cut-out ornaments. We strung long strings of popcorn chains. Crayon Santas and silver-paper wreaths poured out of our assembly line.

In the corner of the room, atop a desk decorated with crepe-paper rosettes, sat our Christmas grab bag. Every kid in the class had bought a gift for the grab bag, with someone's name—drawn from a hat—attached. I had bought for Helen Weathers a large, amazingly life-like, jet-black rubber tarantula. I cackled fiendishly as I wrapped it, and even now its beady green eyes glared from somewhere in the depths of the Christmas grab bag. I knew she'd like it.

Miss Bodkin, after recess, addressed us:

"I want all of you to write a theme. . . ."

A theme! A rotten theme before Christmas! There *must* be kids somewhere who love writing themes, but to a normal air-breathing human kid, writing themes is a torture that ranks only with the dreaded medieval chin-breaker of Inquisitional fame. A theme!

". . . entitled 'What I want for Christmas,' " she concluded.

The clouds lifted. I saw a faint gleam of light at the other end of the black cave of gloom which had enveloped me since my visit to Santa. Rarely had the words poured from my penny pencil with such feverish fluidity. Here was a theme on a subject that needed talking about if ever one did! I remember to this day its glorious winged phrases and concise imagery:

> What I want for Christmas is a Red Ryder BB gun with a compass in the stock and this thing that tells time. I think everybody should have a Red Ryder BB gun. They are very good for Christmas. I don't think a football is a very good Christmas present.

I wrote it on blue-lined paper from my Indian Chief tablet, being very careful about the margins. Miss Bodkin was very snippy about uneven margins. The themes were handed in and I felt somehow that when Miss Bodkin read mine she would sympathize with my plight and make an appeal on my behalf to the powers that be, and that everything would work out, somehow. She was my last hope.

The final day before vacation dawned dank and misty, with swirling eddies of icy wind that rattled the porch swing. Warren G. Harding School glowed like a jeweled oasis amid the sooty snowbanks of the playground. Lights blazed from all the windows, and in every room the Christmas party spirit had kids writhing in their seats. The morning winged by, and after lunch Miss Bodkin announced that the rest of the afternoon would be party time. She handed out our graded themes, folded, with our names scrawled on the outside. A big red *B* in Miss Bodkin's direct hand glowed on my literary effort. I opened it, expecting Miss Bodkin's usual penciled corrections, which ran along the lines of "Watch margins" or "Check Sp." But this time a personal note leaped up, flew around the room, and fastened itself leech-like on the back of my neck:

"You'll shoot your eye out. Merry Christmas."

I sat in my seat, shipping water from every seam. Was there no end to this conspiracy of irrational prejudice against Red Ryder and his peacemaker? Nervously I pulled out of my desk the dog-eared back page of *Open Road For Boys*, which I had carried with me everywhere, waking and sleeping, for the past few weeks. Red Ryder's handsome orange face with the big balloon coming out of his mouth did not look discouraged or defeated. Red must have been a kid once himself, and they must have told him the same thing when he asked for his first Colt .44 for Christmas.

I stuffed my tattered dreams back into my geography book and gloomily watched other, happier, carefree, singing kids who were going to *get* what they wanted for Christmas as Miss Bodkin distributed little green baskets filled with hard candy. Somewhere off down the hall the sixth-grade glee club was singing "Oh little town of Bethlehem, how still we see thee lie. . . ."

Mechanically my jaws crunched on the concrete-hard rock candy and I stared hopelessly out of the window, past cut-out Santas and garlands of red and green chains. It was already getting dark. Night falls fast in Northern Indiana at that time of year. Snow was beginning to fall, drifting softly through the feeble yellow glow of the distant street lamps while around me unbridled merriment raged higher and higher.

By suppertime that night I had begun to resign myself to my fate. After all, I told myself, you can always use another football, and, anyway, there will be other Christmases.

The day before, I had gone with my father and mother to the frozen parking lot next to the Esso station where, after long and soul-searching discussion, we had picked out our tree.

"There's a bare spot on the back."

"It'll fluff out, lady, when it gets hot."

"Is this the kind the needles fall out?"

"Nah, that's them balsams."

"Oh."

Now it stood in the living room, fragrantly, toweringly, teeteringly. Already my mother had begun the trimming operations. The lights were lit, and the living room was transformed into a small, warm paradise.

From the kitchen intoxicating smells were beginning to fill the house. Every year my mother baked two pumpkin pies, spicy and immobilizingly rich. Up through the hot-air registers echoed the boom and bellow of my father fighting The Furnace. I was locked in my bedroom in a fever of excitement. Before me on the bed were sheets of green and yellow paper, balls of colored string, and cellophane envelopes of stickers showing sleighing scenes, wreaths, and angels blowing trumpets. The zeppelin was already lumpily done—it had taken me forty-five minutes—and now I struggled with the big one, the magnificent gleaming gold and pearl perfume atomizer, knowing full well that I was wrapping what would undoubtedly become a treasured family heirloom. I checked the lock on the door, and for double safety hollered:

"DON'T ANYONE OPEN THIS DOOR!"

I turned back to my labors until finally there they were—my masterworks of creative giving piled in a neat pyramid on the quilt. My brother was locked in the bathroom, wrapping the fly swatter he had bought for the Old Man.

Our family always had its Christmas on Christmas Eve. Other less fortunate people, I had heard, opened their presents in the chill clammy light of dawn. Far more civilized, *our* Santa Claus recognized that barbaric practice for what it was. Around midnight great heaps of tissuey, crinkly, sparkly, enigmatic packages appeared among the lower branches of the tree and half hidden among the folds of the white bedsheet that looked in the soft light like some magic snowbank.

Earlier, just after the tree had been finished, my father had taken me and my brother out in the Graham-Paige to "pick up a bottle of wine." When we returned, Santa had been there and gone! On the end table and the bookcase were bowls of English walnuts, cashews, and almonds and petrified hard candy. My brother circled around the tree, moaning softly, while I, cooler and more controlled, quickly eyed the mountain of revealingly wrapped largess—and knew the worst.

Out of the kitchen came my mother, flushed and sparkly-eyed, bearing two wineglasses filled with the special Walgreen drugstore vintage that my Old Man especially favored. Christmas had officially begun. As they sipped their wine we plunged into the cornucopia, quivering with desire and the ecstasy of unbridled avarice. In the background, on the radio, Lionel Barrymore's wheezy, friendly old voice spoke kindly of Bob Cratchit and Tiny Tim and the ghost of old Marley.

The first package I grabbed was tagged "To Randy from Santa." I feverishly passed it over to my brother, who always was a slow reader, and returned to work. Aha!

"To Ralphie from Aunt Clara"—on a largish, lumpy, red-wrapped gift that I suspected to be the crummy football. Frantically I tore off the wrappings. Oh no! OH NO! A pair of fuzzy, pink, idiotic, cross-eyed, lop-eared bunny slippers! Aunt Clara had for years labored under the delusion that I was not only perpetually four years old but also a girl. My mother instantly added oil to the flames by saying:

"Oh, aren't they sweet! Aunt Clara always gives you the nicest presents. Put 'em on; see if they fit."

They did. Immediately my feet began to sweat as those two fluffy little bunnies with blue button eyes stared sappily up at me, and I knew that for at least two years I would have to wear them every time Aunt Clara visited us. I just hoped that Flick would never spot them, as the word of this humiliation could easily make life at Warren G. Harding School a veritable hell.

Next to me in harness my kid brother silently, doggedly stripped package after package until he hit the zeppelin. It was the jackpot!

"WOW! A ZEPPELIN! WHOOPEE! WOW!"

Falling over sideways with an ear-splitting yell, he launched it upward into the middle branches of the tree. Two glass angels and a golden bugle crashed to the floor, and a string of lights winked out.

"It's not supposed to fly, you nut," I said.

"AHH, WHAT GOOD IS A ZEPPELIN THAT DON'T FLY!?"

"It rolls. And beeps."

Instantly he was on his knees pushing the Graf Zeppelin,

beeping fiendishly, propellers clacking, across the living-room rug. It was a sound that was to become sickeningly familiar in the months ahead. I suspect even at that moment my mother knew that one day the zeppelin would mysteriously disappear, never to beep again.

My father was on his feet with the first blink of the dying tree lights. He loved nothing better than to track down the continual short circuits and burned-out bulbs of Christmas tree light strings. Oblivious, I continued to ravage my gifts, feigning unalloyed joy at each lousy Sandy Andy, dump truck, and Monopoly game. My brother's gift to me was the only bright spot in an otherwise remarkably mediocre haul: a rubber Frankenstein face which I knew would come in handy. I immediately put it on and, peering through the slit eyes, continued to open my booty.

"Oh, how terrible!" my mother said. "Take it off and put it away."

"I think it looks good on him," my father said. I stood up and did my already famous Frankenstein walk, clumping stiff-legged around the living room and back to the tree.

Finally it was all over. There were no more mysterious packages under the tree, only a great pile of crumpled tissue paper, string, and empty boxes. In the excitement I had forgotten Red Ryder and the BB gun, but now it all came back. Skunked! Well, at least I had a Frankenstein face. And there was no denying that I had scored heavily with the Simoniz and the atomizer, as well as the zeppelin. The joy of giving can uplift the saddened heart.

My brother lay dozing amid the rubble, the zeppelin clasped in one hand and his new fire truck in the other. My father bent over from his easy chair, his eighth glass of wine in his hand.

"Say, don't I see something over there stuck behind the drapes? Why, I think there *is* something over there behind the drapes."

He was right! There *was* a tiny flash of red under the ecru curtains. Like a shot I was off, and milliseconds later I knew that old Santa had come through! A long, heavy, red-wrapped package, marked "To Ralphie from Santa" had been left somehow behind the curtains. In an instant the wrappings were off, and there it was! A Red Ryder carbine-action range-model BB gun lay in its crinkly white packing, blue-steel barrel graceful and taut, its dark, polished stock gleaming like all the treasures of the Western world. And there, burned into the walnut, his level gaze unmistakable, his jaw clean and hard, was Red Ryder himself coolly watching my every move. His face was even more beautiful and malevolent than the pictures in the advertisements showed.

Over the radio thundered a thousand-voiced heavenly choir:

"JOY TO THE WORLD, THE LORD HAS COME. . . ."

My mother sat and smiled a weak, doubtful smile while my Old Man grinned broadly from behind his wineglass.

The magnificent weapon came equipped with two heavy tubes of beautiful Copproteck BBs, gleaming gold and as hard as sin itself. Covered with a thin film of oil they poured with a "ssshhhing" sound into the 200-shot magazine through a BB-size hole in the side of that long blue-steel tube. They added weight and a feeling of danger to the gun. There were also printed targets, twenty-five of them, with a large bull's-eye inside concentric rings marked "One-Two-Three-Four," and the bull's-eye was printed right in the middle of a portrait of Red Ryder himself.

I could hardly wait to try it out, but the instruction booklet said, in Red Ryder's own words:

> Kids, never fire a BB gun in the house. They can really shoot. And don't ever shoot at other kids. I never shoot anybody but bad guys, and I don't want any of my friends hurt.

It was well past midnight anyway and, excitement or no, I was getting sleepy. Tomorrow was Christmas Day, and the relatives were coming over to visit. That would mean even more loot of one kind or another.

In my warm bed in the cold still air I could hear the falling snow brushing softly against the dark window. Next to me in the blackness lay my oiled blue-steel beauty, the greatest Christmas gift I had ever received. Gradually I drifted off to sleep—pranging ducks on the wing and getting off spectacular hip-shots as I dissolved into nothingness.

Dawn came. As the gray light crept around the shades and over the quilt, I was suddenly and tinglingly awake. Stealthily I dressed in my icy maroon corduroy knickers, my sheepskin coat, and my plaid sweater. I pulled on my high-tops and found my mittens, crept through the dark living room, fragrant with Christmas tree, and out onto the porch. Inside the house the family slept the sleep of the just and the fulfilled.

During the night a great snow had fallen, covering the gritty remains of past snowfalls. The trees hung rich and heavy with fluffy down. The sun, soaring bright and brilliantly sharp over Pulaski's Candy Store, lit up the soft, rolling moonscape of snow with orange and gold splashes of color. Overnight the temperature had dropped thirty degrees or more, and the brittle, crackling air was still and clean, and it hurt the lungs to breathe it. The temperature stood at perhaps fifteen to twenty below zero, cold enough to make the telephone wires creak and groan in agony. From the eaves of the front porch gnarled crystal icicles stretched all the way to the drifts on the buried lawn.

I trudged down the steps, barely discernible in the soft fluff, and now I stood in the clean air, ready to consummate my great, long, painful, ecstatic love affair. Brushing the snow off the third step, I propped up a gleaming Red Ryder target, the black rings and bull's-eye standing out starkly against the snowy whiteness. Above the bull's-eye Red Ryder watched me, his eyes following my every move. I backed off into the snow a good twenty feet, slammed the stock down onto my left kneecap, holding the barrel with my mittened left hand, flipped the mitten off my right and, hooking my fingers in the icy carbine lever, cocked my blue-steel buddy for the first time. I heard the BB click down into the chamber; the spring inside twanged sharply, and with a clunk she rested taut, hard, and loaded in my chapped, rapidly bluing hands.

For the first time I sighted down over that cold barrel, the heart-shaped rear sight almost brushing my nose and the blade of the front sight wavering back and forth, up and down, and finally coming to rest sharply, cutting the heart and laying dead on the innermost ring. Red Ryder didn't move a muscle, his Stetson flaring out above the target as he waited.

Slowly I squeezed the frosty trigger. Back . . . back . . . back. For one instant I thought wildly: It doesn't work! We'll have to send it back! And then:

CRRAAACK!

The gun jerked upward and for a brief instant everything stood still. The target twitched a tiny tick—and then a massive wallop, a gigantic, slashing impact crashed across the left side of my face. My horn-rimmed glasses spun from my head into a snowbank. For several seconds I stood, not knowing what had happened, warm blood trailing down over my cheek and onto the walnut stock of my Red Ryder 200-shot range-model BB gun.

I lowered the barrel convulsively. The target still stood; Red Ryder was unscratched. A ragged, uncontrolled tidal wave of pain, throbbing and singing, rocked my head. The ricocheting BB had missed my eye by perhaps a half inch, and a long, angry, bloody welt extended from my cheekbone almost to my ear. It was divine retribution! Red Ryder had struck again! Another bad guy had been gunned down!

Frantically I scrambled for my glasses. And then the most catastrophic blow of all—they were pulverized! Few things brought such swift and terrible retribution on a kid during the Depression as a pair of busted glasses. The left lens was out as clean as a whistle, and for a moment I thought: I'll fake it! They'll never know the lens is gone! But then, gingerly fingering my rapidly swelling black eye, I realized that here was a shiner on the way that would top even the one I got the time I fought Grover Dill.

As I put the cold horn-rims back on my nose, the front door creaked open just a crack and I could make out the blur of my mother's Chinese-red chenille bathrobe.

"Be careful. Don't shoot out your eye! Just be careful now."

She hadn't seen! Rapidly my mind evolved a spectacular fantasy involving a falling icicle and how it had hit the gun barrel which caused the stock to bounce up and cut my cheek and break my glasses and I tried to get out of the way but the icicle fell off the roof and hit the gun and it bounced up and hit me and. . . . I began to cry uproariously, faking it at first, but then the shock and fear took over and it was the real thing—heaving, sobbing, retching.

I was now in the bathroom, my mother bending over me, telling me:

"There now, see, it's just a little bump. You're lucky you didn't cut your eye. Those icicles sometimes even kill people. You're really lucky. Here, hold this rag on it, and don't wake your brother."

I HAD PULLED IT OFF!

I sipped the bitter dregs of coffee that remained in my cup, suddenly catapulted by a falling tray back into the cheerful, impersonal, brightly lit clatter of Horn & Hardart. I wondered whether Red Ryder was still dispensing retribution and frontier justice as of old. Considering the number of kids I see with broken glasses, I suspect he is.

B-12
19
13
7
8

THE COUNTERFEIT SECRET CIRCLE MEMBER GETS THE MESSAGE, *OR* THE ASP STRIKES AGAIN

Every day when I was a kid I'd drop anything I was doing, no matter what it was—stealing wire, having a fistfight, siphoning gas—no matter what, and tear like a blue streak through the alleys, over fences, under porches, through secret short-cuts, to get home not a second too late for the magic time. My breath rattling in wheezy gasps, sweating profusely from my long cross-country run I'd sit glassy-eyed and expectant before our Crosley Notre Dame Cathedral model radio.

I was never disappointed. At exactly five-fifteen, just as dusk was gathering over the picturesque oil refineries and the faint glow of the muttering Open Hearths was beginning to show red against the gloom, the magic notes of an unforgettable theme song came rasping out of our Crosley:

"Who's that little chatterbox . . . ?
The one with curly golden locks. . . .
Who do I see . . . ?
It's Little Orphan Annie."

Ah, they don't write tunes like that any more. There was one particularly brilliant line that dealt with Sandy, Little Orphan Annie's airedale sidekick. Who can forget it?

Arf goes Sandy.

I think it was Sandy more than anyone else that drew me to the Little Orphan Annie radio program. Dogs in our neighborhood never went "Arf." And they certainly were a lot of things, but never faithful.

Little Orphan Annie lived in this great place called Tompkins Corners. There were people called Joe Corntassle and Uncle. They never mentioned the poolroom. There were no stockyards or fistfights. Or drunks sleeping in doorways in good old Tompkins Corners. Orphan Annie and Sandy and Joe Corntassle were always out chasing pirates or trapping smugglers, neither of which we ever had in Indiana as far as I knew. We had plenty of hubcap stealers and once even a guy who stole a lawn. But no pirates. At least they didn't call them that.

She also had this friend named The Asp, who whenever she was really in a tight spot would just show up and cut everybody's head off. I figured that if there was anything a kid of seven needed it was somebody named The Asp. Especially in our neighborhood. He wore a towel around his head.

Immediately after the nightly adventure, which usually took place near the headwaters of the dreaded Orinoco, on would come a guy named Pierre André, the *definitive* radio announcer.

"FELLAS AND GALS. GET SET FOR A MEETING OF THE LITTLE ORPHAN ANNIE SECRET CIRCLE!"

His voice boomed out of the Crosley like some monster, maniacal pipe organ played by the Devil himself. Vibrant, urgent, dynamic, commanding. Pierre André. I have long had a suspicion that an entire generation of Americans grew up feeling inferior to just the *names* of the guys on the radio. Pierre André. Harlow Wilcox. Vincent Pelletier. Truman Bradley. Westbrook Van Voorhees. André Baruch. Norman Brokenshire. There wasn't a Charlie Shmidlap in the lot. Poor little Charlie crouching next to his radio—a born Right Fielder. Playing right field all of his life, knee-deep in weeds, waiting for a flyball that never comes and more than half afraid that one day they *will* hit one in his direction.

"OKAY, KIDS. TIME TO GET OUT YOUR SECRET DECODER PIN. TIME FOR ANOTHER SECRET MESSAGE DIRECT FROM LITTLE ORPHAN ANNIE TO MEMBERS OF THE LITTLE ORPHAN ANNIE SECRET CIRCLE."

I got no pin. A member of an Out Group at the age of seven. And the worst kind of an Out Group. I am living in a non-Ovaltine-drinking neighborhood.

"ALL RIGHT. SET YOUR PINS TO B-7. SEVEN . . . TWENTY-TWO . . . NINETEEN . . . EIGHT . . . *FORTY-NINE* . . . SIX . . . THIRTEEN . . . *THREE!* . . . TWENTY-TWO . . . ONE . . . FOUR . . . NINETEEN."

Pierre André could get more out of just numbers than Orson Welles was able to squeeze out of *King Lear*.

"FOURTEEN . . . NINE . . . THIRTY-TWO. OKAY, FELLAS AND GALS, OVER AND OUT."

Then—silence. The show was over and you had a sinister feeling that out there in the darkness all over the country there were millions of kids—decoding. And all I could do was to go out into the kitchen where my mother was cooking supper and knock together a salami sandwich. And plot. Somewhere kids were getting the real truth from Orphan Annie. The message. And I had no pin. I lived in an Oatmeal-eating family and listened to an Ovaltine radio show. To get into the Little Orphan Annie Secret Circle you had to send in the silver inner seal from a can of what Pierre André called "that rich chocolate-flavored drink that all the kids love." I had never even *seen* an Ovaltine can in my life.

But as the old truism goes, every man has his chance, and when yours comes you had better grab it. They do not make appointments for the next day. One day while I am foraging my way home from school, coming down one of my favorite alleys, knee-deep in garbage and the thrown-out effluvia of kitchen life, there occurred an incident which forever changed my outlook on Existence itself, although of course at the time I was not aware of it, believing instead that I had struck the Jackpot and was at last on my way into the Big Time.

There was a standard game played solo by almost every male kid I ever heard of, at least in our neighborhood. It was simple, yet highly satisfying. There were no rules except those which the player improvised as he went along. The game had no name and is probably as old as creation itself. It consisted of kicking a tin can or tin cans all the way home. This game is not to be confused with a more formal athletic contest called Kick The Can, which *did* have rules and even teams. This kicking game was a solitary, dogged contest of kid against can, and is quite possibly the very earliest manifestation of the Golf Syndrome.

Anyway, I am kicking condensed milk cans, baked bean cans, sardine cans along the alley, occasionally changing cans at full gallop, when I suddenly found myself kicking a can of a totally unknown nature. I kicked it twice; good, solid, running belts, before I discovered that what I was kicking was an Ovaltine can, the first I had ever seen. Instantly I picked it up, astounded by the mere presence of an Ovaltine drinker in our neighborhood, and then discovered that they had not only thrown out the Ovaltine can but had left the silver inner seal inside. Some rich family had thrown it *all* away! Five minutes later I've got this inner seal in the mail and I start to wait. Every day I would rush home from school and ask:

"Is there any mail for me?"

Day after day, eon after eon. Waiting for three weeks for

something to come in the mail to a kid is like being asked to build the Pyramids singlehanded, using the #3 Erector set, the one without the motor. We never did get much mail around our house anyway. Usually it was bad news when it *did* come. Once in a while a letter marked OCCUPANT arrived, offering my Old Man $300 on his signature only, no questions asked, "Even your employer will not be notified." They began with:

"Friend, are you in Money troubles?"

My Old Man could never figure out how they knew, especially since they only called him OCCUPANT. Day after day I watched our mailbox. On Saturdays when there was no school I would sit on the front porch waiting for the mailman and the sound of the yelping pack of dogs that chased him on his appointed rounds through our neighborhood, his muffled curses and thumping kicks mingling nicely with the steady uproar of snarling and yelping. One thing I knew. Trusty old Sandy never chased a mailman. And if he *had*, he would have caught him.

Everything comes to he who waits. I guess. At last, after at least 200 years of constant vigil, there was delivered to me a big, fat, lumpy letter. There are few things more thrilling in Life than lumpy letters. That rattle. Even to this day I feel a wild surge of exultation when I run my hands over an envelope that is thick, fat, and pregnant with mystery.

I ripped it open. And there it was! My simulated gold plastic Decoder pin. With knob. And my membership card.

It was an important moment. Here was a real milestone,

and I knew it. I was taking my first step up that great ladder of becoming a real American. Nothing is as important to an American as a membership card with a seal. I know guys who have long strings of them, plastic-enclosed: credit cards, membership cards, identification cards, Blue Cross cards, driver's licenses, all strung together in a chain of Love. The longer the chain, the more they feel they belong. Here was my first card. I was on my way. And the best of all possible ways—I was making it as a Phony. A non-Ovaltine drinking Official Member.

> BE IT KNOWN TO ALL AND SUNDRY THAT MR. RALPH WESLEY PARKER IS HEREBY APPOINTED A MEMBER OF THE LITTLE ORPHAN ANNIE SECRET CIRCLE AND IS ENTITLED TO ALL THE HONORS AND BENEFITS ACCRUING THERETO.

Signed: Little Orphan Annie. Countersigned: Pierre André. In ink.

Honors and benefits. Already, at the age of seven, I am *Mister* Parker. They hardly ever even called my Old Man that.

That night I can hardly wait until the adventure is over. I want to get to the real thing, the message. That's what counts. I had spent the entire day sharpening pencils, practicing twirling the knob on my plastic simulated gold Decoder pin. I had lined up plenty of paper and was already at the radio by three-thirty, sitting impatiently through the drone of the late afternoon Soap Operas and newscasts, waiting for my direct contact with Tompkins Corners, my first night as a full Member.

As five-fifteen neared, my excitement mounted. Running waves of goose pimples rippled up and down my spine as I hunched next to our hand-carved, seven-tube Cathedral in the living room. A pause, a station break. . . .

"Who's that little chatterbox. . . .
The one with curly golden locks. . . .
Who do I see . . . ?
It's Little Orphan Annie."

Let's get on with it! I don't need all this jazz about smugglers and pirates. I sat through Sandy's arfing and Little Orphan Annie's perils hardly hearing a word. On comes, at long last, old Pierre. He's one of *my* friends now. I am In. My first secret meeting.

"OKAY, FELLAS AND GALS. GET OUT YOUR DECODER PINS. TIME FOR THE SECRET MESSAGE FOR ALL THE REGULAR PALS OF LITTLE ORPHAN ANNIE, MEMBERS OF THE LITTLE ORPHAN ANNIE SECRET CIRCLE. ALL SET? HERE WE GO. SET YOUR PINS AT B-12."

My eyes narrowed to mere slits, my steely claws working with precision, I set my simulated gold plastic Decoder pin to B-12.

"ALL READY? PENCILS SET?"

Old Pierre was in great voice tonight. I could tell that tonight's message was really important.

"SEVEN . . . TWENTY-TWO . . . THIRTEEN . . . NINETEEN . . . *EIGHT!*"

I struggled furiously to keep up with his booming voice dripping with tension and excitement. Finally:

"OKAY, KIDS, THAT'S TONIGHT'S SECRET MESSAGE. LISTEN AGAIN TOMORROW NIGHT, WHEN YOU HEAR. . . ."

"Who's that little chatterbox. . . .
The one with curly golden locks. . . ."

Ninety seconds later I am in the only room in the house where a boy of seven could sit in privacy and decode. My pin is on one knee, my Indian Chief tablet on the other. I'm starting to decode.

7. . . .

I spun the dial, poring over the plastic scale of letters. Aha! B. I carefully wrote down my first decoded number. I went to the next.

22. . . .

Again I spun the dial. E. . . .

The first word is B-E.

13 . . . S . . .

It was coming easier now.

19 . . . U.

From somewhere out in the house I could hear my kid

brother whimpering, his wail gathering steam, then the faint shriek of my mother:

"Hurry up! Randy's gotta go!" Now what!

"I'LL BE RIGHT OUT, MA! GEE WHIZ!"

I shouted hoarsely, sweat dripping off my nose.

S . . . U . . . 15 . . . R . . . E. BE SURE! A message was coming through!

Excitement gripped my gut. I was getting The Word. BE SURE . . .

14 . . . 8 . . . T . . . O . . . BE SURE TO what? What was Little Orphan Annie trying to say?

17 . . . 9 . . . DR . . . 16 . . . 12 . . . I . . . 9 . . . N . . . K . . . 32 . . . OVA . . . 19 . . . LT . . .

I sat for a long moment in that steamy room, staring down at my Indian Chief notebook. A crummy commercial!

Again a high, rising note from my kid brother.

"I'LL BE RIGHT OUT, MA! FOR CRYING OUT LOUD."

I pulled up my corduroy knickers and went out to face the meat loaf and the red cabbage. The Asp had decapitated another victim.

MY OLD MAN AND THE LASCIVIOUS SPECIAL AWARD THAT HERALDED THE BIRTH OF POP ART

I "hmmmmed" meaningfully yet noncommittally as I feigned interest in the magnificent structure before us. "Hmmmm," I repeated, this time in a slightly lower key, watching carefully out of the corner of my eye to see whether she was taking the lure.

A 1938 Hupmobile radiator core painted gaudily in gilt and fuchsia revolved on a Victrola turntable before us. From its cap extended the severed arm of a female plastic mannequin. It reached toward the vaulted ceiling high above us. Its elegantly contorted hand clutched a can of Bon Ami, the kitchen cleanser. The Victrola repeated endlessly a recording of a harmonica band playing "My Country 'Tis of Thee." The bronze plaque at its base read: IT HASN'T SCRATCHED YET.

The girl nodded slowly and deliberately in deep appreciation of the famous contemporary masterwork, the central exhibit in the Museum's definitive Pop Art Retrospective Panorama, as the Sunday supplements called it. I closed in:

"He's got it down."

I paused adeptly, waited a beat or two and then, using my clipped, put-down voice:

". . . *all* of it."

She rose to the fly like a hungry she-salmon:

"It's The Bronx, all right. Fordham Road, squared. Let 'em laugh *this* off on the Grand Concourse!"

I moved in quickly.

"You can say that again!"

Hissing in the venomous sibilant accents of a lifelong Coffee Shop habitué that I always used in the Museum of Modern Art on my favorite late afternoon time-killer—Girl Tracking—which is the art most fully explored and pursued at the Museum of Modern Art. Nowhere in all of New York is it easier, nor more pleasant, to snare and net the complaisant, rebellious, burlap-skirted, sandal-wearing CCNY undergraduate. Amid the throngs of restless Connecticut matrons and elderly Mittel European art nuts there is always, at the Museum, a roving eddying gulf stream of Hunters and the Hunted.

It was the work of an instant to bundle her off to the outdoor tables in the garden where we sat tensely; date and cream cheese sandwiches between sips of watery Museum of Modern Art orange drink.

"Marcia, how many of these clods *really* dig?" I shrugged toward all the other tables around us. "It's really sickening!!"

"Bastards!"

She whistled through her teeth. I sensed the stirrings, faint but unmistakable, of an Afternoon Love. Up to her pad off the NYU campus, down to the Village by subway for a hamburger, and then. . . .

"Only the other day," she continued, "at the Fig, I said to Claes: 'Pop Shmop. Art is Art, the way I see it'. . . ."

She trailed off moodily and then bit viciously into the raisin nut bread, her Mexican serape sweeping the ashes from her cigarette into my salad.

"Good old Claes." I followed her lead, "He lays it on the Phonies!"

I wondered frantically for a brief instant who the hell Claes was!

"And they lap it up," she added.

Our love duet was meshing nicely now. Point and counterpoint we wove our fabric of Protest, Tristan and Isolde of the Hip.

A light fog-like rain descended on us from what passes for sky in New York. We ignored the dampness as we clutched and groped toward one another in the psychic gloom.

"What do these Baby Machines know of Pop Art?"

I nodded toward a covey of Connecticut ladies eating celery near us. Our eyes met intensely for a long, searing moment. Hers smoldered; mine watered, but I hung in there grimly. And then, her voice low, quivering with emotion, deliberately she spoke:

"Pop Art, as these fools call it, is the essential dissection of Now-ness, the split atom of the Here moment."

We looked deep into each other's souls for another looping instant. I took three deliberate beats and countered:

"Now-ness is US, baby. The *Now* of Here!"

Her hand clutched convulsively at the smudged and dog-eared paperback copy of *Sexus*. A Henry Miller. I knew my harpoon had struck pay dirt!

Suddenly, without warning, she stood up and called out in a loud voice:

"Steve! Oh Stevie, over here!"

I turned and saw striding toward us over the marble palazzo, past a Henry Moore fertility symbol, a tall broad-shouldered figure wearing black cowboy boots and tight leather pants. Marcia hurriedly darted forward.

"I've been waiting, Stevie. You're late."

Stevie, her high cheekbones topped by two angry embers for eyes, snapped:

"Let's go, baby. I'm double-parked. And the fuzz tag a Harley-Davidson around here quicker than a kick in the ass. Let's go."

Her rich bass voice echoed from statue to statue. Marcia, weakly indicating me, said:

"Uh . . . this is . . . uh . . . uh. . . ."

"Pleased ta meetcha, Bud," Stevie barked manfully, her thin moustache bristling in cheery greeting. They were off arm in arm. Once again I was alone amid the world's art treasures.

"You can't win 'em all."

I muttered under my breath as I wolfed down what remained of Marcia's sandwich, salvaging what little I could from the fiasco. The competition for girls in New York is getting rougher and more complex by the moment. I ironically raised my paper cup of tepid orange drink to the gray heavens, sighting over its waxen brim the glowering bronze head of Rodin's *Balzac* outlined craggily against the jazzily lit museum interior, the pink plaster arm of IT HASN'T SCRATCHED YET seeming to reach out of Balzac's neck.

"To good old Claes. And Pop Shmop."

I drained the miserable orange drink with a single strangled gulp. Then it happened. Somewhere way off deep down in that dark, buried coal bin of my subconscious a faint but unmistakable signal squeaked and then was silent. A signal about what? Why? What was Balzac trying to say? Or was it Rodin? Once again I sighted over the statue's head and aligned the mannequin arm at exactly the same position that had set off that faint ringing. The rain drifted down silently while I waited. Nothing.

I tried again; still nothing. My eye fell on Marcia's half-empty cup. Could there be a connection? Carefully realigning the arm and statue, I sipped the sickening liquid. Far off, unmistakably, once again the bell tolled for me. There was no question about it. Unmistakably there was a connection between the orange drink and that arm, not to mention glowering old Balzac, the original woman hater.

By now the rest of the tables had been deserted by my fellow Pop Art lovers. Alone, I sat in the museum garden, contemplating the inexplicable. The pieces began to assemble themselves with no help from me. I slowly began to realize that I had been fortunate enough to be present at the very birth of Pop Art itself. And had, in fact, known intimately the very first Pop Art fanatic who had endured, like all true avant-garde have always, the scorn and jibes of those nearest to them. His dedication to his aesthetic principles almost wrecked our happy home. My father was a full generation ahead of his time, and he never knew it.

The Depression days were the golden age of the newspaper Puzzle Contest. Most newspapers had years before given up the futile struggle to print News, since nothing much ever happened and had turned their pages over to comic strips and endless Fifty Thousand Dollar Giant Jackpot Puzzle Contests. Dick Tracy became a national hero. Andy Gump was more widely quoted than the President. Orphan Annie's editorializing swayed voters by the million. Popeye raised the price of spinach to astronomical heights, and Wimpy spawned a chain of hamburger joints.

As for puzzles, when one ended, another began immediately and occasionally as many as three or four colossal contests ran simultaneously. NAME THE PRESIDENTS, MYSTERY MOVIE STARS, FAMOUS FIGURES IN HISTORY, MATCH THE BABY PICTURES. On and on the contests marched, all variations on the same theme, page after page of distorted and chopped-up pictures of movie stars, kings, novelists, and ballplayers, while in the great outer darkness, for the price of a two-cent newspaper, countless millions struggled nightly to Hit The Jackpot. They were all being judged for Originality, Neatness, and Aptness of Thought. All decisions, of course, were final.

Occasionally the tempo varied with a contest that featured daily a newspaper camera shot taken of a crowd at random—walking across a street, waiting for a light, standing at a bus stop. IS YOUR FACE CIRCLED? IF IT IS, CALL THE HERALD EXAMINER AND CLAIM FIVE HUNDRED DOLLARS!! The streets were full of roving bands of out-of-work contestants, hoping to have their faces circled. My father was no exception. One of his most treasured possessions was a tattered newspaper photo that he carried for years in his wallet, a photo of a crowd snapped on Huron Street that showed, not more than three inches away from the circled face, a smudged figure wearing a straw skimmer, looking the wrong way. He swore it was him. He had invented an involved story to corroborate this, which he told at every company picnic for years.

He was particularly hooked on FIND THE HIDDEN OBJECTS and HOW MANY MISTAKES ARE IN THIS PICTURE?, which consisted of three-legged dogs, ladies with eight fingers, and smokestacks with smoke blowing in three directions. He was much better at this game than the Historical Figures. No one in Hohman had ever even heard of Disraeli, but they sure knew a lot about smokestacks and how many horns a cow had, and whether birds flew upside down or not.

Contest after contest spun off into history. Doggedly my father labored on. Every night the *Chicago American* spread out on the dining-room table, paste pot handy, scissors and ruler, pen and ink, he clipped and glued; struggled and guessed. He was not the only one in that benighted country who pasted a white wig on Theodore Roosevelt and called him John Quincy Adams, or confused Charlemagne with Sitting Bull. But to the faithful and the persevering and to he who waits awards will come. The historic day that my father "won a prize" is still a common topic of conversation in Northern Indiana.

The contest dealt with GREAT FIGURES FROM THE WORLD OF SPORTS. It was sponsored by a soft-drink company that manufactured an artificial orange drink so spectacularly gassy that violent cases of The Bends were common among those who bolted it down too fast. The color of this volatile liquid was a blinding iridescent shimmering, luminous orange that made *real* oranges pale to the color of elderly lemons by comparison. Taste is a difficult thing to describe, but suffice it to say that this beverage, once quaffed, remained forever in the gastronomical memory as unique and galvanic.

All popular non-alcoholic drinks were known in those days by a single generic term—"Pop." What this company made was called simply "Orange pop." The company trademark, seen everywhere, was a silk-stockinged lady's leg, realistically flesh-colored, wearing a black spike-heeled slipper. The knee was crooked slightly and the leg was shown to the middle of the thigh. That was all. No face; no torso; no dress—just a stark, disembodied, provocative leg. The name of this pop was a play on words, involving the lady's knee. Even today in the windows of dusty, fly-specked Midwestern grocery stores and poolrooms this lady's leg may yet be seen.

The first week of the contest was ridiculously easy: Babe Ruth, Bill Tilden, Man O' War, and the Fighting Irish. My Old Man was in his element. He had never been known to read anything *but* the Sport page. His lifetime subscription to the *St. Louis Sporting News* dated back to his teen-age days. His memory and knowledge of the minutia and trivia of the Sporting arenas was deadening. So naturally he whipped through the first seven weeks without once even breathing hard.

Week by week the puzzlers grew more obscure and esoteric. Third-string utility infielders of Second-Division ball clubs, substitute Purdue halfbacks, cauliflower-eared canvas-backed Welterweights, selling platers whose only distinction was a nineteen-length defeat by Man O'War. The Old Man took them all in his stride. Night after night, snorting derisively, cackling victoriously, consulting his voluminous records, he struggled on toward the Semi-Finals.

A week of nervous suspense and a letter bearing the imprint of a lady's leg informed him that he was now among the Elect. He had survived all preliminary eliminations and was now entitled to try for the Grand Award of $50,000, plus "hundreds of additional valuable prizes."

Wild jubilation gripped the household, since no one within a thirty-mile radius had ever gotten this far in a major contest, least of all the Old Man. He usually petered out somewhere along the fourth set of FAMOUS FACES and went back to his Chinese nail puzzle and the ball scores. That night we had ice cream for supper.

The following week the first set of puzzles in the final round arrived in a sealed envelope. They were killers! Even the Old Man was visibly shaken. His face ashen, a pot of steaming black coffee at his side, the kids locked away in the bedroom so as not to disturb his massive struggle, he labored until dawn. The pop company had pulled several questionable underhanded ploys. Water Polo is not a common game in Hohman and its heroes are not on everyone's tongue. Hop Skip & Jump champions had never been lionized in Northern Indiana. No one had even *heard* of Marathon Walking! It was a tough night.

His solutions were mailed off, and again we waited. Another set of even more difficult puzzles arrived. Again the sleepless ordeal, the bitter consultations with poolroom scholars, the sense of imminent defeat, the final hopeless guesses, the sealed envelope. Then silence. Days went by with no word of any kind. Gaunt, hollow-eyed, my father watched the mailman as he went by, occasionally pausing only to drop off the gas bill or flyers offering neckties by mail. It was a nervous, restless time. Sudden flareups of temper, outbursts of unmotivated passion. At night the wind soughed emptily and prophetically through the damp clotheslines of the haunted backyards.

Three weeks to a day after the last mailing, a thin, neat, crisp envelope emblazoned with the sinister voluptuous insignia lay enigmatically on the dining-room table, awaiting my father's return from work. The minute he roared into the kitchen that night he knew.

"It's come! By God! Where is it?"

What had come? Fifty thousand dollars? Fame? A trip to the moon? The end of the rainbow? News of yet another failure?

With palsied hand and bulging eye he carefully slit the crackling envelope. A single typewritten sheet:

> CONGRATULATIONS. YOU HAVE WON A MAJOR AWARD IN OUR FIFTY THOUSAND DOLLAR "GREAT HEROES FROM THE WORLD OF SPORTS" CONTEST. IT WILL ARRIVE BY SPECIAL MESSENGER DELIVERED TO YOUR ADDRESS. YOU ARE A WINNER. CONGRATULATIONS.

That night was one of the very few times my father ever actually got publicly drunk. His cronies whooped and hollered, guzzled and yelled into the early morning hours, knocking over chairs and telling dirty stories. My mother supplied endless sandwiches and constantly mopped up. Hairy Gertz, in honor of the occasion, told his famous dirty story about the three bartenders, the Franciscan monk, and the cross-eyed turtle. Three times. It was a true Victory Gala of the purest sort.

Early the next morning the first trickle of a flood of envy-tinged congratulations began to come in. Distant uncles, hazy second cousins, real estate agents, and Used-Car salesmen called to offer heartfelt felicitations and incidental suggestions for highly rewarding investments they had at their disposal. The Old Man immediately, once his head had partially cleared, began to lay plans. Perhaps a Spanish adobe-type house in Coral Gables, or maybe he'd open up his own Bowling Alley. Victory is heady stuff, and has often proved fatal to the victors.

The next afternoon a large unmarked delivery truck stopped in front of the house. Two workmen unloaded a square, sealed, waist-high cardboard carton, which was lugged into the kitchen. They left and drove off. Somehow an air of foreboding surrounded their stealthy, unexplained operation.

The Old Man, his face flushed with excitement, fumbling in supercharged haste to lay bare his hard-won symbol of Victory, struggled to open the carton. A billowing mushroom of ground excelsior surged up and out. In he plunged. And there it was.

The yellow kitchen light bulb illumined the scene starkly and yet with a touch of glowing promise. Tenderly he lifted from its nest of fragrant straw the only thing he had ever won in his life. We stood silent and in awe at the sheer shimmering, unexpected beauty of the "Major Award."

Before us in the heavy, fragrant air of our cabbage-scented kitchen stood a *life-size* lady's leg, in true blushing-pink flesh tones and wearing a modish black patent leather pump with spike heel. When I say life-size I am referring to a rather large lady who obviously had dined well and had matured nicely. It was a well filled-out leg!

It was so realistic that for a brief instant we thought that we had received in the mail the work of an artist of the type that was very active at that period—the Trunk Murderer. For some reason this spectacular form of self-expression has declined, but in those days something in the air caused many a parson's daughter to hack up her boyfriend into small segments which were then shipped separately to people chosen at random from the phone book. Upon being apprehended and tried, she was almost always acquitted, whereupon she accepted numerous offers to appear in Vaudeville as a featured headliner, recalling her days as a Trunk Murderer complete with props and a dramatized stage version of the deed.

For a split instant it seemed as though our humble family had made the headlines.

My mother was the first to recover.

"What is it?"

"A . . . leg," my father incisively shot back.

It was indeed a leg, more of a leg in fact than any leg any of us had ever seen!

"But . . . what is it?"

"Well, it's a leg. Like a statue, I guess."

"A *statue?*"

Our family had never owned a statue. A statue was always considered to be a lady wearing a wreath and concrete robes, holding aloft a torch in one hand and a book in the other. This was the only kind of statue outside of generals sitting on horses that we had ever heard about. They all had names like VICTORY or PEACE. And if this was a statue, it could only have one name:

WHOOPEE!

My mother was trying to get herself between the "statue" and the kids.

"Isn't it time for bed?"

"Holy Smokes, would you look at that!"

My father was warming up.

"Holy Smokes, would you *look* at that? Do you know what this is?"

My mother did not answer, just silently edged herself between my kid brother and the magnificent limb.

"Would you believe it, it's a LAMP!"

It was indeed a lamp, a lamp in its own way a *Definitive* lamp. A master stroke of the lightoliers' art. It was without question the most magnificent lamp that we had ever seen.

This was the age of spindly, artificially antiqued, teetery brass contrivances called "bridge lamps." These were usually of the school of design known as WPA Neo-Romanticism, a school noted for its heavy use of brass flower petals and mottled parchment shades depicting fauns and dryads inscribed in dark browns and greens. The light bulbs themselves were often formed to emulate a twisted, spiraled candle flame of a peculiar yellow-orange tint. These bulbs were unique in that they contrived somehow to make a room even dimmer when they were turned on. My mother was especially proud of her matched set, which in addition to brass tulip buds teetered shakily on bases cleverly designed to look like leopards' paws.

On the kitchen table stood the lamp that was destined to play a subtle and important role in our future. My Old Man dove back into the box, burrowing through the crackling packing.

"AHA! Here's the shade!"

A monstrous, barrel-shaped bulging tube of a shade, a striking Lingerie pink in color, topped by a glittering cut-crystal orb, was lifted reverently up and put onto the table. Never had shade so beautifully matched base. Within an instant the Old Man had screwed it atop the fulsome thigh, and there it stood, a full four feet from coquettishly pointed toe to sparkling crystal. His eyes boggled behind his Harold Lloyd glasses.

"My God! Ain't that great? Wow!!"

He was almost overcome by Art.

"What a great lamp!"

"Oh . . . I don't know."

My mother was strictly the crocheted-doily type.

"What a great lamp! Wow! This is exactly what we need for the front window. Wow!"

He swept up the plastic trophy, his symbol of Superiority, and rushed out through the dining room and into the living room. Placing the lamp squarely in the middle of the library table, he aligned it exactly at the center of the front window. We trailed behind him, applauding and yipping. He was unrolling the cord, down on all fours.

"Where's the damn plug?"

"Behind the sofa."

My mother answered quietly, in a vaguely detached tone.

"Quick! Go out in the kitchen and get me an extension!"

Our entire world was strung together with "extensions." Outlets in our house were rare and coveted, each one buried under a bakelite mound of three-way, seven-way, and ten-way plugs and screw sockets, the entire mess caught in a twisted, snarling Gordian knot of frayed and cracked lamp cords, radio cords, and God knows what. Occasionally in some houses a critical point was reached and one of these electrical bombs went off, sometimes burning down whole blocks of homes, or more often blowing out the main fuse, plunging half the town into darkness.

"Get the extension from the toaster!"

He shouted from under the sofa where he was burrowing through the electrical rat's nest.

I rushed out into the kitchen, grabbed the extension, and scurried back to the scene of action.

"Give it to me! Quick!"

His hand reached out from the darkness. For a few moments—full silence, except for clickings and scratchings. And deep breathing from behind the sofa. The snap of a few sparks, a quick whiff of ozone, and the lamp blazed forth in unparalleled glory. From ankle to thigh the translucent flesh radiated a vibrant, sensual, luminous orange-yellow-pinkish nimbus of Pagan fire. All it needed was tom-toms and maybe a gong or two. And a tenor singing in a high, quavery, earnest voice:

"A pretty girl/Is like a melody. . . ."

It was alive!

"Hey, look."

The Old Man was reading from the instruction pamphlet which had been attached to the cord.

"It's got a two-way switch. It says here: 'In one position it's a tasteful Night Light and in the other an effective, scientifically designed Reading Lamp.' Oh boy, is this great!"

He reached up under the shade to throw the switch.

"Why can't you wait until the kids are in bed?"

My mother shoved my kid brother behind her. The shade had a narrow scallop of delicate lace circling its lower regions.

"Watch this!"

The switch clicked. Instantly the room was flooded with a wave of pink light that was pure perfume of illumination.

"Now that is a real lamp!"

The Old Man backed away in admiration.

"Hey wait. I want to see how it looks from the outside."

He rushed into the outer darkness, across the front porch and out onto the street. From a half block away he shouted:

"Move it a little to the left. Okay. That's got it. You oughta see it from out here!"

The entire neighborhood was turned on. It could be seen up and down Cleveland Street, the symbol of his victory.

The rest of that evening was spent in honest, simple Peasant admiration for a thing of transcendent beauty, very much like the awe and humility that we felt before such things as Christmas trees and used cars with fresh coats of Simonize. The family went to bed in a restless mood of festive gaiety. That is, everyone except my mother, who somehow failed to vibrate on the same frequency as my father's spectacular Additional Major Award.

That night, for the first time, our home had a Night Light. The living room was bathed through the long, still, silent hours with the soft glow of electric Sex. The stage was set; the principal players were in the wings. The cue was about to be given for the greatest single fight that ever happened in our family.

Real-life man and wife, mother and father battles rarely even remotely resemble the Theatrical or Fictional version of the Struggle between the Sexes. Homes have been wracked by strife and dissension because of a basic difference of opinion over where to go on a vacation, or what kind of car to buy, or a toaster that made funny noises, or a sister-in-law's false teeth, not to mention who is going to take out the garbage. And why.

In all my experience I have never known homes that had the kind of fights that appear in plays by Edward Albee and

Tennessee Williams. It would never have occurred to my father to bellow dramatically in the living room, after twenty-seven Scotches:

"You bitch! You're not going to emasculate *me!*"

The Old Man would not have even known what the word "emasculate" *meant*, much less figure that that's what my mother was up to.

On the other hand, my mother thought "emasculation" had something to do with women getting the vote. But, in any event, Sex is rarely argued and fought over in any household *I* ever heard of, outside of heaving novels and nervous plays. That was not the kind of fights we had at home. There was no question of Emasculation or Role Reversal. My mother was a *Mother*. She knew it. My Old Man was . . . the Old Man. *He* knew it. There was no problem of Identity, just a gigantic clash of two opposing physical presences: the Immovable Body and the Force That Is Not To Be Denied.

The lamp stood in the middle of the window for months. Every night my mother would casually, without a word, draw the curtains shut, while Bing Crosby sang from the old Gothic Crosley:

"Hail KMH/Hail to the foe
Onward to victory/Onward we must go. . . ."

the theme song of the Kraft Music Hall. The Old Man would get up out of his chair. Casually. He would pull the curtain back, look out—pretending to be examining the weather—and leave it that way. Ten minutes later my mother would get up out of her chair, casually, saying:

"Gee, I feel a draft coming in from somewhere."

This slowly evolving ballet spun on through the Winter months, gathering momentum imperceptively night after night. Meanwhile, the lamp itself had attracted a considerable personal following among cruising prides of pimply-faced Adolescents who night after night could hardly wait for darkness to fall and the soft, sinuous radiation of Passion to light up the drab, dark corners of Cleveland Street.

The pop company enjoyed sales of mounting intensity, even during the normally slack Winter months. Their symbol now stood for far more than a sickeningly sweet orange drink that produced window-rattling burps and cavities in Adolescent teeth of such spectacular dimensions as to rival Mammoth Cave. Night after night kids' eyes glowed in the darkness out on the street before our house, like predatory carnivores of the jungle in full cry. Night after night the lady's leg sent out its silent message.

The breaking point came, as all crucial moments in History do, stealthily and on cats' feet, on a day that was notable for its ordinariness. We never know when lightning is about to strike, or a cornice to fall. Perhaps it is just as well.

On the fateful day I came home from school and immediately opened the refrigerator door, looking for Something To Eat. Seconds later I am knocking together a salami sandwich. My Old Man—it was his day off—is in the john. Hollering, as he always did, accompanied by the roar of running water, snatches of song, complaints about No Pressure—the usual. My mother is somewhere off in the front of the house, puttering about. Dusting.

Life is one long song. The White Sox have won a ball game, and it's only spring training. The Old Man is singing. My brother is under the daybed, whimpering. The salami is as sweet as life itself.

The first fireflies were beginning to flicker in the cottonwoods. Northern Indiana slowly was at long last emerging from the iron grip of the Midwestern Winter. A softness in the air; a quickening of the pulse. Expectations long lying dormant in the blackened rock ice of Winter sent out tentative tender green shoots and yawned toward the smoky sun. Somewhere off in the distance, ball met bat; robin called to robin, and a screen door slammed.

In the living room my mother is talking to the aphids in her fern plant. She fought aphids all of her life. The water roared. I started on a second sandwich. And then:

CAAA-RAASHH!

". . . oh!" A phony, stifled gasp in the living room.

A split second of silence while the fuse sputtered and ignited, and it began.

The Old Man *knew*. He had been fearing it since the very first day. The bathroom door slammed open. He rushed out, dripping, carrying a bar of Lifebuoy, eyes rolling wildly.

"What broke!? What happened?! WHAT BROKE!!?"

". . . the lamp." A soft, phony voice, feigning heartbreak.

For an instant the air vibrated with tension. A vast magnetic charge, a static blast of human electricity, made the air sing. My kid brother stopped in mid-whimper. I took the last bite, the last bite of salami, knowing that this would be my last happy bite of salami forever.

The Old Man rushed through the dining room. He fell heavily over a footstool, sending a shower of spray and profanity toward the ceiling.

"Where is it? WHERE IS IT!?"

There it was, the shattered kneecap under the coffee table, the cracked, well-turned ankle under the radio; the calf—that voluptuous poem of feminine pulchritude—split open like a rotten watermelon, its entrails of insulated wire hanging out limply over the rug. That lovely lingerie shade, stove in, had rolled under the library table.

"Where's my glue? My glue! OH, MY LAMP!"

My mother stood silently for a moment and then said:

"I . . . don't know what happened. I was just dusting and . . . ah. . . ."

The Old Man leaped up from the floor, his towel gone, in stark nakedness. He bellowed:

"YOU ALWAYS WERE JEALOUS OF THAT LAMP!"

"Jealous? Of a *plastic leg?*"

Her scorn ripped out like a hot knife slicing through soft oleomargarine. He faced her.

"You were jealous 'cause I WON!"

"That's ridiculous. Jealous! Jealous of what? That was the ugliest lamp I ever saw!"

Now it was out, irretrievably. The Old Man turned and walked to the window. He looked out silently at the soft gathering gloom of Spring. Suddenly he turned and in a flat, iron voice:

"Get the glue."

"We're *out* of glue," my mother said.

My father always was a superb user of profanity, but now he came out with just one word, a real Father word, bitter and hard.

"DAMMIT!"

Without another word he stalked into the bedroom; slammed the door, emerged wearing a sweatshirt, pants and shoes, and his straw hat, and out he went. The door of the Oldsmobile slammed shut out in the driveway.

"K-runch. Crash!"—a tinkle of glass. He had broken the window of the one thing he loved, the car that every day he polished and honed. He slammed it in Reverse.

RRRRAAAWWWWWRRRRR!

We heard the fender drag along the side of the garage. He never paused.

RRRRAAAWWWWWRRROOOOMMMM!

And he's gone. We are alone. Quietly my mother started picking up the pieces, something she did all her life. I am hiding under the porch swing. My kid brother is now down in the coal bin.

It seemed seconds later:

BBBRRRRRRAAAAAWWWRRRRR . . . eeeeeeeeeh!

Up the driveway he charged in a shower of cinders and

burning rubber. You could always tell the mood of the Old Man by the way he came up that driveway. Tonight there was no question.

A heavy thunder of feet roared up the back steps, the kitchen door slammed. He's carrying three cans of glue. Iron glue. The kind that garage mechanics used for gaskets and for gluing back together exploded locomotives. His voice is now quiet.

"Don't touch it. *Don't touch that lamp!*"

He spread a newspaper out over the kitchen floor and carefully, tenderly laid out the shattered fleshy remains. He is on all fours now, and the work began. Painfully, hopelessly he tried to glue together the silk-stockinged, life-size symbol of his great victory.

Time and again it looked almost successful, but then he would remove his hand carefully. . . . BOING! . . . the kneecap kept springing up and sailing across the kitchen. The ankle didn't fit. The glue hardened into black lumps and the Old Man was purple with frustration. He tried to fix the leg for about two hours, stacking books on it. A Sears Roebuck catalog held the instep. The family Bible pressed down on the thigh. But it wasn't working.

To this day I can still see my father, wearing a straw hat, swearing under his breath, walking around a shattered plastic lady's leg, a Freudian image to make Edward Albee's best efforts pale into insignificance.

Finally he scooped it all up. Without a word he took it out the back door and into the ashbin. He sat down quietly at the kitchen table. My mother is now back at her lifelong station, hanging over the sink. The sink is making the Sink noise. Our sink forever made long, gurgling sighs, especially in the evening, a kind of sucking, gargling, choking retch.

Aaaagggghhhh—and then a short, hissing wheeze and silence until the next attack. Sometimes at three o'clock in the morning I'd lie in my bed and listen to the sink—Aaaaaggggghhhh.

Once in a while it would go: gaaaaaggggghhhh . . . PTUI! —and up would come a wad of Mrs. Kissel's potato peelings from next door. She, no doubt, got our coffee grounds. Life was real.

My mother is hanging over her sink, swabbing eternally with her Brillo pad. If mothers had a coat of arms in the Midwest, it would consist of crossed Plumbers' Helpers rampant on a field of golden Brillo pads.

The Old Man is sitting at the kitchen table. It was white enamel with little chipped black marks all around the edge. They must have been made that way, delivered with those flaws. A table that smelled like dishrags and coffee grounds and kids urping. A kitchen-table smell, permanent and universal, that defied all cleaning and disinfectant—the smell of Life itself.

In dead silence my father sat and read his paper. The battle had moved into the Trench Warfare or Great Freeze stage. And continued for three full days. For three days my father spoke not. For three days my mother spoke likewise.

There was only the sink to keep us kids company. And, of course, each other, clinging together in the chilly subterranean icy air of a great battle. Occasionally I would try.

"Hey Ma, ah . . . you know what Flick is doing . . . uh. . . ."

Her silent back hunched over the sink. Or:

"Hey Dad, Flick says that. . . ."

"WHADDAYA WANT?"

Three long days.

Sunday was sunny and almost like a day in Midsummer. Breakfast, usually a holiday thing on Sundays, had gone by in stony silence. So had dinner. My father was sitting in the living room with the sun streaming in unobstructed through the front window, making a long, flat, golden pattern on the dusty Oriental rug. He was reading Andy Gump at the time. My mother was struggling over a frayed elbow in one of my sweaters. Suddenly he looked up and said:

"You know. . . ."

Here it comes! My mother straightened up and waited.

"You know, I like the room this way."

There was a long, rich moment. These were the first words spoken in seventy-two hours.

She looked down again at her darning, and in a soft voice:

"Uh . . . you know, I'm sorry I broke it."

"Well . . ." he grew expansive, "it was . . . it was really pretty jazzy."

"No," she answered, "I thought it was very *pretty!*"

"Nah. It was too pink for this room. We should get some kind of brass lamp for that window."

She continued her darning. He looked around for a moment, dropped the Funnies noisily to get attention, and then announced in his Now For The Big Surprise voice:

"How 'bout let's all of us going to a movie? How 'bout it? Let's all take in a movie!"

Ten minutes later we're all in the Oldsmobile, on our way to see Johnny Weissmuller.

The drizzle had become a full rain by the time I realized I was the only one left in the windswept garden of the Museum of Modern Art. The lights were on inside, warm and glowing, and I could see a pink arm reaching skyward. I went back in to have another last, loving look at IT HASN'T SCRATCHED YET.

GROVER DILL AND THE TASMANIAN DEVIL

The male human animal, skulking through the impenetrable fetid jungle of Kidhood, learns early in the game just what sort of animal he is. The jungle he stalks is a howling tangled wilderness, infested with crawling, flying, leaping, nameless dangers. There are occasional brilliant patches of rare, passionate orchids and other sweet flowers and succulent fruits, but they are rare. He daily does battle with horrors and emotions that he will spend the rest of his life trying to forget or suppress. Or recapture.

His jungle is a wilderness he will never fully escape, but those first early years when the bloom is on the peach and the milk teeth have just barely departed are the crucial days in the Great Education.

I am not at all sure that girls have even the slightest hint that there *is* such a jungle. But no man is really qualified to say. Most wildernesses are masculine, anyway.

And one thing that must be said about a wilderness, in contrast to the supple silkiness of Civilization, is that the basic, primal elements of existence are laid bare and raw. And can't be ducked. It is in that jungle that all men find out about themselves. Things we all know, but rarely admit. Say, for example, about that beady red-eyed, clawed creature, that ravening Carnivore, that incorrigibly wild, insane, scurrying little beast—the Killer that is in each one of us. We pretend it is not there most of the time, but it is a silly idle sham, as all male ex-kids know. They have seen it and have run fleeing from it more than once. Screaming into the night.

One quiet Summer afternoon, leafing through a library book, with the sun slanting down on the oaken tables, I came across a picture in a Nature book of a creature called the Tasmanian Devil. He glared directly at me out of the page, with an unwavering red-eyed gaze, and I have never forgotten it. I was looking at my soul!

The Tasmanian Devil is well named, being a nocturnal marsupial of extraordinary ferocity, being strictly carnivorous, and when cornered fighting with a nuttiness beyond all bounds of reason. In fact, it is said that he is one of the few creatures on earth that *looks forward* to being cornered.

I looked him in the eye; he looked back, and even from the flat, glossy surface of the paper I could feel his burning rage, a Primal rage that glowed white hot like the core of a nuclear explosion. A chord of understanding was struck between us. He knew and I knew. We were Killers. The only thing that separated us was the sham. He admitted it, and I have been attempting to cover it up all of my life.

I remember well the first time my own Tasmanian Devil without warning screamed out of the darkness and revealed himself for what he was—a fanged, maniacal meat eater. Every male child sweats inside at a word that is rarely heard today: the Bully. That is not to say that bullies no longer exist. Sociologists have given them other and softer-sounding labels, an "over-aggressive child," for example, but they all amount to the same thing—Meatheads. Guys who grow up banging grilles in parking lots and becoming captains of Industry or Mafia hatchet men. Every school had at least five, and they usually gathered followers and toadies like barnacles on the bottom of a garbage scow. The lines were clearly drawn. You were either a Bully, a Toady, or one of the nameless rabble of Victims who hid behind hedges, continually ran up alleys, ducked under porches, and tried to get a connection with City Hall, City Hall being the Bully himself.

I was an accomplished Alley Runner who did not wear sneakers to school from choice but to get off the mark quicker. I was well qualified to endorse Keds Champions with:

"I have outrun some of the biggest Bullies of my time wearing Keds, and I am still here to tell the tale."

It would make a great ad in *Boys' Life*:

> "KIDS! When that cold sweat pours down your back and you are facing the Moment Of Truth on the way home from the store, don't you wish you had bought Keds? Yes, our new Bully-Beater model has been endorsed by skinny kids with glasses from coast to coast. That extra six feet may mean the difference between making the porch and you-know-what!"

Many of us have grown up wearing mental Keds and still ducking behind filing cabinets, water coolers, and into convenient men's rooms when that cold sweat trickles down between the shoulder blades. My Moment of Truth was a kid named Grover Dill.

What a rotten name! Dill was a Running Nose type of Bully. His nose was *always* running, even when it wasn't. He was a yelling, wiry, malevolent, sneevily snively Bully who had quelled all insurgents for miles around. I did not know one kid who was not afraid of Dill, mainly because Dill was truly aggressive. This kind of aggression later in life is often called "Talent" or "Drive," but to the great formless herd of kids it just meant a lot of running, getting belted, and continually feeling ashamed.

If Dill so much as said "Hi" to you, you felt great and warm inside. But mostly he just hit you in the mouth. Now a true Bully is not a flash in the pan, and Dill wasn't. This went on for years. I must have been in about second grade when Dill first belted me behind the ear.

Maybe the terrain had something to do with it. Life is

very basic in Northern Indiana. Life is more Primal there than in, say, New York City or New Jersey or California. First of all, Winters are really *Winters* there. Snow, ice, hard rocky frozen ground that doesn't thaw out until late June. Kids played baseball all Winter on this frozen lumpy tundra. Ground balls come galloping: "K-tunk K-tunk K-tunk K-tunk" over the Arctic concrete. And then summer would come. The ground would thaw and the wind would start, whistling in off the Lake, a hot Sahara gale. I lived the first ten years of my life in a continual sandstorm. A sandstorm in the Dunes region, with the temperature at 105 and no rain since the first of June, produces in a kid the soul of a Death Valley prospector. The Indiana Dunes—in those days no one thought they were special or spectacular—they were just the Dunes, all sand and swamps and even timber wolves. There were rattlesnakes in the Dunes, and rattlesnakes in fifth grade. Dill was a Puff-Adder among garden worms.

This terrain grew very basic kids who fought the elements all their lives. We'd go to school in a sandstorm and come home just before a tornado. Lake Michigan is like an enormous flue that stretches all the way up into the Straits of Mackinac, into the Great North Woods of Canada, and the wind howls down that lake like an enormous chimney. We lived at the bottom of this immense stovepipe. The wind hardly ever stops. Winter, Spring, Summer, Fall—whatever weather we had was made twenty times worse by the wind. If it was warm, it seared you like the open door of a blast furnace. If it was cold, the wind sliced you to little pieces and then put you back together again and sliced you up the other way, then diced and cubed you, ground you up, and put you back together and started all over again. People had red faces all year round from the wind.

When the sand is blowing off the Dunes in the Summer, it does something to the temper. The sand gets in your shoes and always hurts between the toes. The kids would cut the sides of their sneakers so that when the sand would get too much, just stick your foot up in the air and the sand would squirt out and you're ready for another ten minutes of action. It breeds a different kind of kid, a kid whose foot is continually cut. One time Kissel spent two entire weeks with a catfish hook in his left heel. He couldn't get it out, so he just kept going to school and walked with one foot in the air. One day Miss Siefert insisted that he go down and see the school nurse, who cut the hook out. Kissel's screaming and yelling could be heard all over the school. So you've got the picture of the Jungle.

Grover Dill was just another of the hostile elements of Nature, like the sand, the wind, and the stickers. Northern Indiana has a strange little green burr that has festered fingers and ankles for countless centuries. One of the great moments in life for a kid was to catch a flyball covered with a thick furr of stickers in a barehand grab, driving them in right to the marrow of the knuckle bones.

One day, without warning of any kind, it happened. Monumental moments in our lives are rarely telegraphed. I am coming home from school on a hot, shimmering day, totally unaware that I was about to meet face to face that Tasmanian Devil, that clawed, raging maniac that lurks inside each of us. There were three or four of us eddying along, blown like leaves through vacant lots, sticker patches, asphalt streets, steaming cindered alleys and through great clouds of Indiana grasshoppers, wading through clouds of them, big ones that spit tobacco juice on your kneecaps and hollered and yelled in the weeds on all sides. The eternal locusts were shrieking in the poplars and the Monarch butterflies were on the wing amid the thistles. In short, it was a day like any other.

My kid brother is with me and we have one of those little running ball games going, where you bat the ball with your hand back and forth to each other, moving homeward at the same time. The traveling game. The ball hops along; you field it; you throw it back; somebody tosses it; it's grabbed on the first bounce, you're out, but nobody stops moving homeward. A moving ball game. Like a floating crap game.

We were about a block or so from my house, bouncing the ball over the concrete, when it happened. We are moving along over the sandy landscape, under the dark lowering clouds of Open-Hearth haze that always hung between us and the sun. I dart to my right to field a ground ball. A foot lashes out unexpectedly and down I go, flat on my face on the concrete road. I hit hard and jarring, a bruising, scraping jolt that cut my lip and drew blood. Stunned for a second, I look up. It is the dreaded Dill!

To this day I have no idea how he materialized out of nowhere to trip me flat and finally to force the issue.

"Come on, kid, get out of the way, will ya?" He grabs the ball and whistles it off to one of his Toadies. He had yellow eyes. So help me God, yellow eyes!

I got up with my knees bleeding and my hands stunned and tingling from the concrete, and without any conception at all of what I was doing I screamed and rushed. My mind a total red, raging, flaming blank. I know I screamed.

"YAAAAAAHHHH!"

The next thing I knew we are rolling over and over on the concrete, screaming and clawing. I'm out of my skull! I am pounding Dill against the concrete and we're rolling over and over, battering at each other's faces. I was screaming continually. I couldn't stop. I hit him over and over in the eyes. He rolled over me, but I was kicking and clawing, gouging, biting, tearing. I was vaguely conscious of people coming out of houses and down over lawns. I was on top. I grabbed at his head. I caught both of Grover Dill's ears in either hand and I began to pound him on the concrete, over and over again.

I have since heard of people under extreme duress speaking in strange tongues. I became conscious that a steady torrent of obscenities and swearing was pouring out of me as I screamed. I could hear my brother running home, hysterically yelling for my mother, but only dimly. All I knew is that I was tearing and ripping and smashing at Grover Dill, who fought back like a fiend! But I guess it was the first time he had ever met face to face with an unleashed Tasmanian Devil.

I continued to swear fantastically, as though I had no control over it. I was conscious of it and yet it was as though it was coming from something or someone outside of me. I swore as I have never sworn since as we rolled screaming on the ground. And suddenly we just break apart. Dill, the back of his head all battered, his eyes puffed and streaming, slashed by my claws and fangs, was hysterical. There was hardly a scratch on me, except for my scraped knees and cut lip.

I learned then that Bravery does not exist. Just a kind of latent Nuttiness. If I had thought about attacking Dill for ten seconds before I had done it, I'd have been four blocks away in a minute flat. But something had happened. A wire broke. A fuse blew. And I had gone out of my skull.

But I had sworn! Terribly! Obscenely! In our house kids didn't swear. The things I called Dill I'm sure my mother had not even heard. And *I* had only heard once or twice, coming out of an alley. I had woven a tapestry of obscenity that as far as I know is still hanging in space over Lake Michigan. And my mother had heard!

Dill by this time is wailing hysterically. This had never happened to him before. They're dragging the two of us apart amid a great ring of surging grownups and exultant, scared kids who knew more about what was happening than the mothers and fathers ever would. My mother is looking at me. She said:

"What did you say?"

That's all. There was a funny look on her face. At that instant all thought of Grover Dill disappeared from what was left of my mind and all I could think of was the incredible shame of that unbelievable tornado of obscenity I had sprayed over the neighborhood.

I go into the house in a daze, and my mother's putting water on me in the bathroom, pouring it over my head and dabbing at my eyes which are puffed and red from hysteria. My kid brother is cowering under the dining-room table, scared. Kissel, next door, has been hiding in the basement, under the steps, scared. The whole neighborhood is scared, and so am I. The water trickles down over my hair and around my ears as I stare into the swirling drainage hole in the sink.

"You better go in and lie down on the daybed. Take it easy. Just go in and lie down."

She takes me by the shoulder and pushes me down on the daybed. I lie there scared, really scared of what I have done. I felt no sense of victory, no sense of beating Dill. All I felt was this terrible thing I had said and done.

The light was getting purple and soft outside, almost time for my father to come home from work. I'm just lying there. I can see that it's getting dark, and I know that he's on his way home. Once in a while a gigantic sob would come out, half hysterically. My kid brother by now is under the sink in the john, hiding among the mops, mewing occasionally.

I hear the car roar up the driveway and a wave of terror breaks over me, the terror that a kid feels when he knows that retribution is about to be meted out for something that he's been hiding forever—his rottenness. The basic rottenness has been uncovered, and now it's the Wrath of God, which you are not only going to get but which you deserve!

I hear him in the kitchen now. I'm in the front bedroom, cowering on the daybed. The normal sounds—he's hollering around with the newspaper. Finally my mother says:

"Come on, supper's ready. Come on, kids, wash up."

I painfully drag myself off the daybed and sneak along the woodwork, under the buffet, sneaking, skulking into the bathroom. My kid brother and I wash together over the sink. He says nothing.

Then I am sitting at the kitchen table, toying with the red cabbage. My Old Man looks up from the Sport page:

"Well, what happened today?"

Here it comes! There is a short pause, and then my mother says:

"Oh, not much. Ralph had a little fight."

"Fight? What kind of fight!"

"Oh, you know how kids are," she says.

The axe is poised over my naked neck! There is no way out! Mechanically I continue to shovel in the mashed potatoes and red cabbage, the meat loaf. But I am tasting nothing, just eating and eating.

"Oh, it wasn't much. I gave him a talking to. By the way, I see the White Sox won today. . . ."

About two thirds of the way through the meal I slowly began to realize that I was not about to be destroyed. And then a very peculiar thing happened. A sudden unbelievable twisting, heaving stomach cramp hit me so bad I could feel my shoes coming right up through my ears.

I rushed back into the bathroom, so sick to my stomach that my knees were buckling. It was all coming up, pouring out of me, the conglomeration of it all. The terror of Grover Dill, the fear of yelling the things that I had yelled, my father coming home, my obscenities . . . I heaved it all out. It poured out of me in great heaving rushes, splattering the walls, the floor, the sink. Old erasers that I had eaten years before, library paste that I had downed in second grade, an Indian Head penny that I had gulped when I was two! It all came up in thunderous, retching heaves.

My father hovered out in the hall, saying:

"What's the matter with him? What's the matter? Let's call Doctor Slicker!"

My mother *knew* what was the matter with me.

"Now he's going to be all right. Just take it easy. Go back and finish eating. Go on."

She pressed a washrag to the back of my neck. "Now take it easy. I'm not going to say anything. Just be quiet. Take it easy."

Down comes the bottle of Pepto-Bismol and the spoon. "Take this. Stop crying."

But then I *really* started to cry, yelling and blubbering. She was talking low and quiet to me.

"We'll tell him your stomach is upset, that you ate something at school."

The Pepto-Bismol slides down my throat, amid my blubbering. It is now really coming out! I'm scared of Grover Dill again, scared of everything. I'm convinced that I will never grow up to be twenty-one, that I'm going blind!

I'm lying in bed, sobbing, and I finally drifted off to sleep, completely passed out from sheer nervous exhaustion. The soft warm air blew the curtains back and forth as we caught the tail of a breeze from the Great North Woods, the wilderness at the head of the Lake. Both of us slept quietly, me and my little red-eyed, fanged, furry Tasmanian Devil. Both of us slept. For the time being.

THE GRANDSTAND PASSION PLAY OF DELBERT AND THE BUMPUS HOUNDS

" 'Mah-ree Elena, yore the answer to mah prayer. . . .' " The familiar twangy moan of old Gene Autry seemed to be coming from next to my ear. It was the first time I had ever dreamed in sound. Or *was* I dreaming?

"FER CHRISSAKE, WHAT THE HELL IS THAT RACKET?" The bedsprings clattered in the next room, as my old man cursed and leaped out of the sack, his feet thumping the floor in the dark. Instantly, I was wide awake.

" 'MAH-REE ELENA. . . .' " It was even louder, now that my mind was working again. The tinny plunking of a guitar cut through the darkness. My kid brother sat up in his bed across the room from me and began to whine, his usual reaction to any outside stimulus.

A guttural grunt of intense pain, followed by a high-pitched bleating wail, as the old man once again unerringly cracked his big toe against the leg of the dresser. He had done this so many times in the past, in the dark, that all the varnish was now worn off the leg, and my father's toe was permanently shaped like a small tennis ball.

"Now what?" My mother joined in the chorus, her hair curlers rattling in the gloom.

" 'WHEN IT'S TWAALAHT ON THE TRAY-ULL. . . .' " Autry had launched into another favorite of simple-minded millions everywhere.

"What the hell *time* is it?" muttered the old man. He was always an aggressive sleeper. Sleep was one of the things he did best, and he loved it. Some look upon sleep as an unfortunately necessary interruption of life; but there are others who hold that sleep *is* life, or at least one of the more fulfilling aspects of it, like eating or sex. Any time my old man's sleep was interrupted, he became truly dangerous.

"It's almost three-thirty. Who the hell's playing those goddamn records at three-thirty?"

Someone was, indeed, playing records at full blast. It was then that we first became aware of another sound—one that was to become more familiar and ominous in the weeks to come: a kind of snuffling, scratching, moiling, squealing, squishy turmoil.

" '. . . THAT SILVUHH HAI-UHD DAH-DEE OF MAHN. . . .' " Doors slammed. Twangy voices argued indistinctly. Gene Autry keened on and on. The snuffling squeals rose and fell. The old man reconnoitered silently through the bedroom curtains.

"HOOIICKK-PATOOOEY!" Something juicy splatted against the side of our house.

"Holy Christ!" The old man hissed a rhetorical comment to no one in particular.

"GRRAAAHHKKK! BROWWK!" A window-rattling burp boomed out over the scratchy Gene Autry disc.

My mother was finally galvanized into action. She had fought a lifelong battle against obscene noises of every variety. I could hear her pattering feet, as she joined my father at the window.

"Who *are* they?" she asked, after a pause to survey the scene.

"Damned if I know!" the old man answered; but I could tell from the sound of his voice that he knew trouble had arrived. Big trouble. The Bumpus crowd had moved in next door and was already in business.

Ours was not a genteel neighborhood, by any stretch of the imagination. Nestled picturesquely between the looming steel mills and the verminously aromatic oil refineries and encircled by a colorful conglomerate of city dumps and fetid rivers, our northern Indiana town was and is the very essence of the Midwestern industrial heartland of the nation. There was a standard barbershop bit of humor that said it with surprising poeticism: If Chicago (only a stone's throw away across the polluted lake waters) was Carl Sandburg's "City of the Broad Shoulders," then Hohman had to be that city's broad rear end.

According to legend, it bore the name of a hapless early

settler who had arrived on the scene when the land was just prairie and Indian trails. Surveying the sparkling blue waters of Lake Michigan, he decided that Chicago, then a tiny trading post where land was free for the asking, had no future. Struggling through the quagmires farther south, for some demented reason now lost to history, he set up camp and invested heavily in land that was destined to become one of the ugliest pieces of real estate this side of the craters of the moon. Indeed, it bore some resemblance to the moon, in that the natives were alternately seared by stifling heat in the summer and reduced to clanking hulks when the fierce gales blew off the lake. Our founding father set the pattern of futility for all future generations.

My old man, my mother, my kid brother and I slogged along in the great tradition. The old man had his high point every Wednesday at George's Bowling Alley, where he once rolled a historic game in which he got three consecutive strikes. My kid brother's nose ran steadily, winter and summer. My mother made red cabbage, peanut-butter-and-jelly sandwiches, meat loaf and Jell-O in an endless stream. And I studied the principal exports of Peru at the Warren G. Harding School.

Delbert Bumpus entered Warren G. Harding like a small, truculent rhinoceros. His hair grew low down on his almost nonexistent forehead, and he had the greatest pair of ears that Warren G. Harding had ever seen, extending at absolutely right angles from his head. Between those ears festered a pea-sized but malevolent brain that almost immediately made him the most feared kid below sixth grade.

He had a direct way of settling disagreements that he established on the second day of his brief but spectacular period at W.G.H. Grover Dill—our number-two-ranking thug, right behind Scut Farkas, who stood alone as the premier bully of all he surveyed—challenged Bumpus to a showdown the first time he laid eyes on those peculiarly provocative ears. It was recess time and, as usual, we milled about aimlessly in the stickers and sand hills of our playground. It was too early for baseball; football had been over for months; we didn't have a basketball hoop; so we just milled.

Spotting Bumpus in his worn blue jeans and black turtleneck—tiny, close-set eyes almost invisible under a thatch of jet-black, wiry hair—Dill opened negotiations, his own slitted eyes glinting in anticipation of a little action:

"What's yer name, kid?"

Bumpus pulled his head lower into the turtleneck and said nothing.

"I SAID, WHAT'S YER NAME, KID?" This time in a loud, trumpeting voice that alerted the rest of the school ground that spring had come and Grover Dill felt the sap rising. Bumpus, a full head and a half shorter than Dill but built along the lines of a fireplug, muttered:

"Bumpus." It was the first word we had heard from him, his accent redolent of the deepest Kentucky hills.

"BUMPUS! What the hell kind of a name is that? Holy Moses! Didja hear that? Bumpus! What kind of a name is that?"

Dill's humor, while extremely primitive, was refreshingly direct. He began to sing in a high, feminine voice:

"Bumpus Schlumpus, double Crumpus—" He broke off, advancing on Bumpus, sandy hair abristle.

"D'ya have a first name, runt?"

Farkas watched with Olympian disinterest as his protégé moved in for the kill. Schwartz huddled next to me, ashen-faced, while Flick attempted to blend into the sand. There wasn't one of us who had not, at one time or another, been dealt with by either Farkas or Dill.

"I said, what's yer first name, kid?" Bumpus, backed up flat against the school wall, finally spoke up:

"Delbert."

"Delbert! *DEL*BERT!" Outraged by such a name, Dill addressed the crowd, with scorn dripping from his every word. "*Delbert Bumpus!* They're letting *everybody* in Harding School these days! What the hell kind of a name is that? That must be some kind of *hillbilly* name!"

It was the last time anyone at Warren G. Harding ever said, or even thought, anything like that about Delbert Bumpus.

Everything happened so fast after that that no two accounts of it were the same. The way I saw it, Bumpus' head snapped down low between his shoulder blades. He bent over from the waist, charged over the sand like a wounded wart hog insane with fury, left his feet and butted his black, furry head like a battering-ram into Dill's rib cage, the sickening thump sounding exactly like a watermelon dropped from a second-story window. Dill, knocked backward by the charge, landed on his neck and slid for three or four feet, his face alternating green and white. His eyes, usually almost unseen behind his cobra lids, popped out like a tromped-on toad-frog's. He lay flat, gazing paralyzed at the spring sky, one shoe wrenched off his foot by the impact. The schoolyard was hushed, except for the sound of a prolonged gurling and wheezing as Dill, now half his original size, lay retching. It was obvious that he was out of action for some time.

Bumpus glared around at the hushed faces, then spit a long stream of rich-brown tobacco juice onto Dill's left tennis shoe. The buzzer sounded for the end of recess, but it was the beginning of a new era.

That's the way the whole Bumpus crowd was, in one way or another. Overnight, the entire neighborhood changed. The Taylors, a quiet family who had lived next to us for years, had moved out and—without warning—the Bumpuses had flooded in. There were thousands of them! The house seemed to age in one week. What had been a nondescript bungalow became a battered, hinge-sprung, sagging hillbilly shack.

I remember only brief images of various Bumpuses. They never mixed with anyone else in the neighborhood, just moiled around, hawking, guffawing, kicking their dogs and piling up junk in the back yard. They drove an old slat-sided Chevy pickup truck that was covered with creamy-white bird droppings and a thick coating of rutted Kentucky clay. It had no windshield and the steering wheel looked like it was made entirely of old black friction tape. It roared like a tank, sending up clouds of blue smoke as it burned the sludge oil that the Bumpuses slopped into it. It seemed to be always hub-deep in mud, even though there was no mud in our neighborhood.

Old Emil Bumpus was kind of the headman. He was about eight feet tall and always walked like he was leaning into a strong wind, with his head hanging down around his overall tops. He must have weighed about 300 pounds, not including his chaw of navy plug, which he must have been born chewing. His neck was so red that at first we thought he always wore some kind of bandanna. But he didn't. He had an Adam's apple that rode up and down the front of his neck like a yo-yo. His hair, which was mud-colored, stuck out in all directions and looked like it had been chopped off here and there with a pair of hedge-trimming shears. And his hands, which hung down to just below his knees, had knuckles the size of pool balls, and there was usually a black, string bandage around a thumb. His hands were made for hitting things.

The Bumpuses weren't in town three days before Emil cleaned out the whole back room at the Blue Bird Tavern one night. They said somebody had given him a dirty look.

Another time, Big Rusty Galambus, who had heard about that incident and felt his reputation was at stake, busted Emil's gallon jug over the back of his head. They said that Emil didn't even know he'd been hit for a couple of minutes, until somebody told him. Then he turned around, stood up, looked down at Big Rusty and said:

"Ah'd be mo' careful with that thar jug a mahn ef'n ah was yew. Ef ah didn' know bettuh, ah mighta tho't yew was spoilin' for a fight."

There was something about the way he said it that persuaded Rusty, a scarred veteran of the open hearth, who had once hoisted the back end of a Ford truck with his bare hands when the jack busted, to apologize and say that the jug slipped.

Emil let it pass; after all, he had 9000 more jugs at home, of all sizes and shapes, sitting on various window sills. We wondered what they were for, until we saw the Bumpuses carrying in pieces of copper tubing—and until we got our first whiff of a mighty aroma from their basement that overpowered even the normal neighborhood smell from the Sinclair oil refinery a half mile away. It got so bad at times that starlings would sit around on the telephone wires back of the Bumpus house, just breathing deeply and falling off into the bushes and squawking. From time to time, there would be a dull explosion in the cellar, and a Bumpus would run out of the house with his overalls on fire.

One afternoon, with a snootful of whatever they were

making down there, Emil came reeling out onto the back porch. He was yelling at somebody in the kitchen, his deep molasses drawl booming out over the neighborhood.

"WHO YEW THANK YO' TAWKIN' TEW?" With that, he grabbed ahold of the back porch and pulled it right off the house. He just grabbed the porch and yanked it out by the roots:

"AAAuuuggghhh!"

From that day on, the Bumpus house had no back porch, only a door about eight feet up in the air and a rusty screen. Once in a while, one of them would jump out—and land in the garbage. And every so often, one of the skinny, red-faced sisters would fall out accidentally, usually carrying a pail of dishwater or chicken innards.

"Lawd a'mighty. Amy Jo, ef'n yew cain't watch them clodhoppers a yourn, we gonna have to chain yew up!" Another raucous round of harrooping. They sure loved one another.

From the day they moved in, the house was surrounded by a thick swamp of junk: old truck tires, barrels full of bottles and tin cans, black oil drums, rusty pitchforks, busted chicken crates, an old bathtub, at least 57 ancient bedsprings, an old tractor hood, a half-dozen rotting bushel baskets overflowing with inner tubes and galoshes, a wheelbarrow with one handle, eight or nine horse collars and a lot of things that nobody could figure out—things that looked like big tall water boilers with pipes sticking out. For some reason, they loved wire; they had all kinds of it—chicken wire, baling wire and rolls of barbed wire, just sort of lying around. And in between the big stuff, there was all the little stuff: sardine cans, old batteries, tire irons, old blue tin cups, corncobs, leather straps and a lot of tire pumps. They were always bringing home license plates, which they nailed up by the basement door. The Bumpuses went to the city dump two or three times a week—like art patrons to a gallery—to stock up on more of the same.

The sea of wreckage spread like a blight onto the surrounding yards, first an ironing board on our lawn, then a bicycle tire in our bushes, then a few odd corncobs on the front porch. And one day, a gust of wind covered my mother's flapping laundry—her pride and joy—with a thin, indelible coating of chicken dung, pigeon feathers, rabbit fur and goat droppings. After that, her jaw was grim, her eyes thin slits of rage, every time another burst of hawkings or blattings reminded her of the Bumpuses. The night my old man tripped in the dark over a rusty radiator in our back yard, causing him to drop his bowling ball on his left foot, didn't help things, either. He grabbed the radiator and flung it into the dark, back into the Bumpuses' yard; it crashed into the rubble, and for five minutes, an avalanche of sound rumbled on and on, like Fibber McGee's closet. Emil stuck his head out of the kitchen window, quickly followed by the barrel of his trusty shotgun. When the old man stood his ground, Emil hissed, "Sic 'em, Luke!" Instantly, 17 dogs roared out from behind the garage. The old man barely made the kitchen.

A few days later, Schwartz, Kissel, Flick and I were

trudging up our driveway when Flick stopped in his tracks, pointed and said, with a touch of delighted wonder, "Hey, look at that funny little house."

"Yeah, look at that little moon on it," replied Schwartz, likewise with some wonder.

"What the hell is it?" Junior Kissel chimed in.

Suddenly, Delbert Bumpus shot around the side of the house, dodging his way through the junk yard like a broken-field runner, and hurled himself headlong into the tiny pine shack and slammed the door, disappearing from our view—but not, unfortunately, beyond our earshot. It was then that we found out about little houses with moons, a new concept for all of us. Devout believers in eternal verities and ancient traditions, the Bumpuses obviously distrusted newfangled, citified contraptions such as that white-porcelain doohickey beside their upstairs bathtub, which didn't get much use, either—except, rumor had it, for the aging and storage of white lightning. From that day on, there was an endless stream of Bumpuses beating a path through the back yard at all hours of the day and night. The outhouse also solved for them the problem of what to do with last year's Sears, Roebuck catalog.

With the Bumpuses—and the outhouse—came the rats. They must have brought back a couple of thousand from one of their trips to the dump. Emil would squat out in back and pop at them with a long-barreled single-shot .22. You could hear the ricochets bouncing off the oil drums, and then Emil yelling:

"Gahdamn, Ima Pearl, ah missed that varmint agin."

"Emil, yew kin go out huntin' after supper. It's time we et."

The Bumpus hounds, who had their own problems with an even larger population of ticks and lice, had no interest at all in the rats. Once in a while, you'd see a hound sprawled flat on his back in the dust, legs spraddled, ears spread out, mouth hanging open, tongue lolling, sound asleep in the sun, with a rat lying beside him like they were the best of friends. The rats had no such nonaggression treaty with the Bumpus chickens, whom they ganged up on now and then, but their losses were too heavy to make it a regular thing. The Bumpuses had *mean* chickens. One big gray hen with a ratty tail and demented yellow eyes chased Schwartz all the way to school one day and waited in the playground for him to come out at recess. He wisely cowered in the locker room.

They also had rabbits—and pigeons. For some reason, hillbillies dearly love pigeons. They kept them in chicken-wire pens when they weren't out dive-bombing our yard and roosting on everybody's laundry. And the Bumpuses had one animal nobody could identify. It was kind of round, with blackish fur and claws. It weighed about 30 pounds or so, and Mrs. Kissel told my mother it was "a swamp bear." Nobody believed her, until one time it tried to eat Mrs. Gammie's Airedale, Rags, who had a nervous breakdown and had to be sent to the country. But the only atrocity it ever actually committed was to devour all my mother's iris bulbs. Emil used to holler at it once in a while, when it got to chewing on the truck tires. Its name was Jack.

The three goats never gave anybody much trouble; in fact, they kept our lawn mowed for us. They didn't smell too good if you got downwind of them on a warm day, but nobody complained about it—what with all the other indescribable smells that drifted our way day and night. My old man would peek out of the kitchen window with a Montgomery Ward spyglass to try to see what the Bumpuses ate when they were all squatting around the trough in the kitchen, with a yellow light bulb hanging overhead amid the wriggling flypaper. There was one smell that really used to get him. He could never tell what it was—a kind of smoky, greasy, gamy animal scent. Then one night he got it. He was watching them wolf it down, the way they always did, slurping and crunching, throwing off a thick yellow spray.

"By God, they're eating possum! That's what it is. Possum!"

My mother, who was always interested in cooking, asked: "Possum, what's that?"

A *Field & Stream* subscriber, the old man immediately answered, "Possum—you know, it's kind of a big rat." My mother, who was putting tomato paste on top of our meat loaf at the time, dropped her spoon and ran into the bathroom. After that, she didn't ask much about what the Bumpuses ate.

"I wonder where the hell they get it?" the old man continued. "I never heard of a possum around here." Where they got possum was just another of the Bumpus mysteries.

Every five minutes or so, someone threw something out

the back window into the yard. My mother would be standing at the sink, peering out the window that looked right into the Bumpus house just across the driveway from us. A soggy paper sack filled with coffee grounds and apple cores would sail out and land amid the rubble.

"Tch, tch, just look at those pigs!"

She was right. We were living next door to a tightly knit band of total slobs, a genuine gypsy family. The Bumpuses were so low down on the evolutionary totem pole that they weren't even included in Darwin's famous family tree. They had inbred and ingrown and finally emerged from the Kentucky hills like some remnant of Attila the Hun's barbarian horde. Flick said that they had webbed feet and only three toes. It might have been true.

Delbert Bumpus, the runt of the litter, came to school about three days a month. It was three times too often. Whenever he showed up, there would be a lot of yelling, and they'd throw him out. Delbert never played with anybody and he hardly ever talked; but he spat a lot. Since he lived with the goats and rabbits and chickens, he didn't smell exactly like the rest of us, either—and *we* weren't any bargain.

One time, Miss Parsons, our gym teacher, made the mistake of putting Delbert in a volleyball game. I guess they never played volleyball in Kentucky, because at first he didn't seem to understand what was going on. But when he got the hang of it, everything changed. He stood there, watching them knock the ball back and forth, for maybe five minutes, and then somebody hit one toward him. He left the ground about three feet and gave the ball an overhand shot that sent it screaming over the net; it caught Schwartz just below the left eye and knocked him flat. Bumpus' side cheered.

Miss Parsons said, "No, Delbert, you mustn't hit it that hard."

Bumpus spat on the gym floor and glared at her for a minute, and then growled, "What the goddamn hell is this game 'spose ta be about?"

While Schwartz crawled around on the floor, crying, Miss Parsons—who taught Sunday school at the Baptist church—tried again.

"You mustn't use those bad words, Delbert. Now, let's begin the game again, shall we?"

Miss Parsons believed in law and order. Schwartz, who had been removed to the nurse's office, trailing blood, had been replaced by Roger Beanblossom, who, at the age of seven, was already six feet tall. Beanblossom, famous for his serve, sliced a whistler right at Bumpus, who stopped scratching just in time to slam the ball back over the net. This time, he got Jack Morton in the pit of his stomach, knocking the wind out of him like a deflated beach ball. He slumped to the floor, the color of Cream of Wheat.

"No, Delbert." Miss Parsons was back in the fray. "Here, I'll show you."

She tapped the ball delicately into the air, to show how the game was played. Bumpus, watching this exhibition, came out with a line that soon became legend at Warren G. Harding School.

"Who the hell wants to play a goddamn silly girl's game lahk that?"

Miss Parsons, now beet red and faced with a question many of us had privately asked, since volleyball was a hated game among the males of the school, could do only one thing. "Delbert Bumpus, you go to the office this instant!"

Picking his nose, Delbert slouched toward the door and muttered, with classic simplicity: "Screw you."

And he left. It was lucky that Miss Parsons didn't know what he meant by that, or there would have been real trouble. He was kicked out of school for only a week.

Then there was the time Miss Shields opened up the day by reading us a chapter of *Raggedy Ann and Raggedy Andy*. Miss Shields was tall and thin and wore rimless glasses. She was a very kind lady, who believed that all children were basically good.

"Boys and girls," she began, after setting the book down, "are there any questions?"

Bumpus, who had never asked a question, spoke up. He had a very deep voice for a kid; already it sounded a lot like old Emil's, rich and phlegmy.

"Yeah." That was all he said.

"Oh, you have a question, Delbert?" asked Miss Shields, obviously pleased. She felt at long last she was *reaching* him.

"Yeah." He was a kid of few words.

"Well, what is your question, Delbert?"

"Was this guy Raggedy Andy a bohunk?"

"What was that?" Miss Shields was caught off guard.

"Mah Uncle Cletus knew a bohunk onc't named Andy."

Miss Shields, who did not know Delbert Bumpus the way the class did, gamely replied: "Well, no, Delbert, Raggedy Andy was not of Bohemian extraction. He was a doll."

"Well, ah'll be goddamned," he snorted.

"What was that, Delbert?" Miss Shields felt the class slipping from her grasp.

"You mean a doll that walked aroun'? Shee-it!"

"Delbert, you mustn't use words like that in class. Yes, Raggedy Andy was a doll who walked around, and so was Raggedy Ann."

Delbert snorted again in disbelief and, as he sat down, said in a loud voice, "Ah nevah did heah such a crock a hog drippin's."

"Delbert," said Miss Shields with an ashen face, "report to the office this instant!" We waited for him to say what he usually said when he left the room, but I guess he liked Miss Shields. He just stalked out and went home.

The only time Delbert ever said anything to me directly was one day when I made the mistake of throwing him out at first base. He looked at me real hard for a long time and then said: "Doan' worry, piss-ant, ah'll git yew someday."

Little did I dream at the time what form his revenge would take.

Delbert was the only Bumpus kid in my grade, but they

infested Warren G. Harding like termites in an outhouse. There was Ima Jean, short and muscular, who was in the sixth grade, when she showed up, but spent most of her time hanging around the poolroom. There was a lanky, blue-jowled customer they called Jamie, who ran the still and was the only one who ever wore shoes. He and his brother Ace, who wore a brown fedora and blue work shirts, sat on the front steps at home on the Fourth of July, sucking at a jug and pretending to light sticks of dynamite with their cigars when little old ladies walked by. There were also several red-faced girls who spent most of their time dumping dishwater out of windows. Babies of various sizes and sexes crawled about the back yard, fraternizing indiscriminately with the livestock. They all wore limp, battleship-gray T-shirts and nothing else. They cried day and night.

We thought that was all of them—until one day a truck stopped in front of the house and out stepped a girl who made Daisy Mae look like Little Orphan Annie. My father was sprinkling the lawn at the time; he wound up watering the windows. Ace and Emil came running out onto the porch, whooping and hollering. The girl carried a cardboard suitcase—in which she must have kept all her underwear, if she owned any—and wore her blonde hair piled high on her head; it gleamed in the midday sun. Her short muslin dress strained and bulged. The truck roared off. Ace rushed out to greet her, bellowing over his shoulder as he ran:

"MAH GAWD! HEY, MAW, IT'S CASSIE! SHE'S HOME FROM THE REFORMATORY!"

Emil grabbed her suitcase and Cassie, the ripest 16-year-old ever to descend on northern Indiana, kissed her father in a way that clouded up windows for blocks around.

"Mah Gawd, Cassie, yew sure filled out!" he boomed, slapping her none too paternally on the backside. Maw Bumpus, drying her hands on her apron, yelled from the porch:

"YEW GIT IN HERE, CASSIE, AN' LEAVE YORE PAW ALONE. LEASTWAYS TILL WE'VE ET."

After that, my father stepped up his spyglass work considerably, since they had no window shades and Cassie liked to dress very casually around the house. She also liked to lie in the swing on the front porch and suck jawbreakers when the weather was hot.

On Saturday nights, even before Cassie arrived, a roaring fleet of old cars would park around the Bumpus house and a mob of slope-browed, slack-jawed friends and relatives would crowd into the place. All night, paneless windows needlessly flung wide, a thunderous square dance would shake the crockery for blocks around. Hawking and spitting and swilling applejack, they yelled and sweated and thumped up and down, while old Emil sat in a corner and sawed on his fiddle. On those nights, hardly anyone dared leave their homes. These parties always ended one way—with a sudden crash, a prolonged scuffle and then:

"EF'N YEW LAY ANOTHA FINGA ON MAH WOMAN, AH'LL SLICE YEW UP LIKE HOG BACON!"

"YEW AN' WHO ELSE, YEW SONOVABITCH!?"

Followed by screams, crashing bottles, running feet; then a distant wail of sirens. A tremendous roaring of ancient motors, a cloud of gravel and they were all gone, leaving a trail of blood and sweat behind them.

Then there were the dogs. They had at least 745 dogs. Now, our neighborhood had always had dogs—walking-around, ordinary dogs, with names like Zero and Ralph. Once in a while, one of them would knock over a garbage can, but they were dogs that knew their place. The Bumpus hounds, on the other hand, didn't seem to be dogs at all, or maybe they were such *total* dogs that no one knew how to handle them. They were the most uninhibited animals you ever saw in your life. They had absolutely no sense of privacy. They did everything in the bright sunlight, and I mean *everything*. They were just a great churning mass of tails and tongues and flea-bitten bodies. You could almost see the smell. On a warm day, a sort of bluish-greenish-yellowish haze hung over the Bumpus house, and even the haze had fleas.

Every day, one of the Bumpus women would swing down from the back door to feed them. She strode amid the slavering pack, carrying a greasy dishpan full of obscene table scraps and chicken gizzards.

"COME AN' GIT YO' VITTLES!"

The mob would charge, rolling over her in a tidal wave of heaving flanks, bloodshot eyes and mangy fur. Snarling and squealing, they stormed over the littered back yard, a heaving ball of yapping curs. The Bumpus woman, fastidiously shifting her wad of tobacco from one side of her mouth to the other, would then kick her way through the pack and back into the house.

They dug holes continuously—under the porch, in the back yard, in the middle of our scrawny lawn and under the car. Five of them took up residence beneath our garage. They slept there in shifts 24 hours a day. Every time the old man would drive the Olds in, we'd hear under the floor: "ROWFF OUFFF ROWWFF!" and they'd run in mad circles around the garage.

"Shoo! Beat it! Lemme alone!" my father would shout, as he hopped up and down amid the hounds, fighting his way toward the kitchen door. We'd see the eyes of the Bumpus family peering out, waiting for him to make a wrong move. They were a real hillbilly family when it came to their dogs. You could say anything you wanted about anybody in the family, but you didn't dare insult one of their dogs. You didn't say anything against Old Blue or Big Red. *All* the dogs—with the exception of those 17 named Luke—were named either Big Red or Old Blue.

Half a dozen times a week, my old man would come sprinting up the back steps just a stride ahead of the leader of the pack—a wiry, scarred battler named, of course, Big Red—baying the way Kentucky hounds always do when they've got a bear up a tree. Every time this would happen, there would be another wave of juicy guffaws and wheezy backslapping from the Bumpus mob. This really burned the old man up. After a hard day at the office and the Olds' acting up again, fighting off Big Red to get into the kitchen really got him. He'd sit at the kitchen table, his face sweaty, gulping down a bottle of Atlas Praeger. Finally, after catching his breath, he'd say, "Goddamn it, did you see what those lousy hounds did to the hedge?"

My mother, who had long since given up caring, always shrugged her shoulders and continued stoically scouring her pots.

When there was a full moon, the Bumpus hounds, feeling some ancient canine urge, would treat the neighborhood to a nightlong serenade.

"OwwwwwwOOOOOOOOOOOOOOO. WOWOOOOOOOOOOOOoooooooooo. Yap yap yaoooOOOOOOoooooooooo."

One after the other, they would take solos; then, after a blessed moment of silence, a full chorus, 15 or 20 strong, would howl to the inconstant moon:

"Yipe yipe yaaWOOOOOOOOOoooooooo. Ow Ow OWOOOOOOO. OOOOOOOooooooWOWOOO WOW! WOW! WOWOOOooooooo."

All over the neighborhood, in darkened bedrooms, hairs rose on reddened necks, children whimpered in fear. The Bumpus hounds bayed on, interspersed with Gene Autry—"MEXICALI ROSE, KEEP SMILIN', AH'LL COME BACK TO YEW . . ."—and the running commentary of the Bumpuses themselves: "HOICK-PATOOEY."

Months went by. We were in a state of siege. Only after you've lived next to a family like the Bumpuses can you understand how anyone could carry on a lifelong feud with his neighbors. My mother and father were just standard-type people. The old man would flip his cork once in a while when the furnace went on the fritz; he'd threaten to blow out his brains when the White Sox traded away the only ballplayer they had. But he never got mad enough to throw rocks at people—not until that fantastic day when the rumbling volcano of his temper, roused from dormancy by the arrival of the Bumpuses, finally erupted.

Every three of four months—roughly three times a year—we would make a major food investment. I suppose rich families don't even think about this kind of thing, but ordinary families in those days spent their lives eating canned corn, meat loaf, peanut-butter sandwiches, oatmeal, red cabbage and peas. In such a home, the great meals that came along every few months stuck out like icebergs in the Caribbean. Buying a turkey was a state occasion. The entire family would go to the market to inspect all the turkeys; they'd discuss the relative merits of each, press the breastbones down, wiggle the legs, until finally they'd take a vote and decide on this particular 12-pounder, which is borne home with honor and prepared for the big day, like a virgin for the sacrifice. It's a ritual almost as cherished and time-honored as the moment when the tribe hunkers around the ceremonial campfire to devour it.

For weeks afterward, the theological debates continue: "That was a very good turkey. Very good."

"It was almost as good as the turkey we had in Thirty-three."

"But it wasn't quite as tender as the one we had in Twenty-nine. Actually, this year's was a little dry."

These feast days are always associated with major holidays: turkey for Thanksgiving and Christmas, roast chicken for birthdays and, in our house, Easter always meant ham. My father was totally ape over ham. The week before Easter, usually on Friday night, he'd say, "I'll tell you what let's do. What do you say we all pile in the car, drive down to the A.&P. and pick out a great big ham for Easter?"

He said it almost nonchalantly, but his eyes would be lit with a wild and ravenous light. It was no small thing he was suggesting, since "a great big ham" meant about half his pay check in those days.

My mother almost always would come back with, "Well, gee, I don't know. Can we afford it this year? We can always get a nice little pot roast."

"Ah, come on! What the hell. You only live once. What do you say?" And she would always relent.

Quivering slightly, he would throw on his coat and rush to the door. He could already see the ham half eaten, rich and red, weeks of magnificent pickings. Nothing goes with Atlas Praeger like cold ham after a session at the bowling alley.

We'd race to the A.&P. All the hams would be laid out, wrapped in white paper, some marked Armour Star, others Swift; not to mention Hormel. There were always great arguments as to which was really best. These were not dinky little canned hams but weighty monsters smoked darkly and tied with greasy, twisted twine.

The old man would go up and down the case, poking, peering, hefting, sniffing, occasionally punching, until, eventually, *the* ham was isolated from the common herd. Somehow, it looked a little different from the rest. It was *our* ham.

We would leave the market with at least four giant bags of groceries, our fare for the week: loaves of Wonder Bread, Campbell's tomato soup, Ann Page pork and beans, eggs, a two-pound jar of grape jelly, fig bars, oatmeal, Cream of Wheat—real *people* food—and the ham. *The* ham.

When we got the ham home, my mother immediately stripped off the white paper and the string in the middle of our chipped white-enamel kitchen table. There it lay, exuding heavenly perfumes—proud, arrogant, regal. It had a dark, smoked, leathery skin, which my mother carefully peeled off with her sharpened bread knife. Then the old man, the only one who could lift the ham without straining a gut, placed it in the big dark-blue oval pot that was used only for hams. My mother then covered the ham with water, pushed it onto the big burner and turned up the gas until it boiled. It just sat there on the stove and bubbled away for maybe two hours, filling the house with a smell that was so luscious, so powerful as to have erotic overtones. The old man paced back and forth, occasionally lifting the lid and prodding the ham with a fork, inhaling deeply. The ham frenzy was upon him.

After about an hour, the whole neighborhood knew what we were having for Easter. Finally, the next phase began. Grunting and straining, my mother poured off the water into another pot. It would later form the base of a magnificent pea soup so pungent as to bring tears to the eyes. She then sprinkled a thick layer of brown sugar, dotted with butter, over the ham. She stuck cloves in it in a crisscross design, then added several slices of Del Monte pineapple, thick and juicy, and topped it off with a maraschino cherry in the center of each slice. She then sprinkled more brown sugar over the lot, a few teaspoons of molasses, the juice from the pineapple can, a little salt, a little pepper, and it was shoved into the oven. Almost instantly, the brown sugar melted over the mighty ham and mingled with the ham juice in the pan.

By this time, the old man, humming nervously to himself, had checked his carving set several times, to make sure the knife was honed, the fork tines sharp—while in the oven, the ham baked on and on, until late Saturday night, when my mother finally turned off the gas, leaving the oven unopened and the ham inside. She said, as she always did, "Never eat a baked ham right after it's baked. Let it sit in the oven for twelve hours at least."

All night long, I would lie in my bed and smell the ham. The next day was Easter: Easter eggs and chocolate bunnies and all that. But the ham and only the ham was what really counted—not only for itself but because it always put my father in a great mood. We would play catch tomorrow; he would drink beer and tell stories. For once, the Bumpuses would be forgotten. Who the hell cares about a bunch of hillbillies, when there's baked him on the table? I lay in my bed, awake, the dark, indescribable aroma of ham coiling sinuously into my bedroom from the kitchen. In the next room, my father snored lustily, resting up for the great feast.

Immediately after breakfast the next morning, while my brother and I crawled around the house, looking for Easter eggs, my mother turned on the oven to heat the ham ever so slowly. This is important, she told us. The flame must be very low.

By 1:30 that afternoon, the tension had risen almost to the breaking point. The smell of ham saturated the drapes. And on my trip down to Pulaski's for the Sunday paper, I found that it could be smelled at least four blocks away. Finally, at about two o'clock, we all gathered around while my mother opened the blue pot—releasing a blast of fragrance so overwhelming that my knees wobbled—and surrounded the ham with sliced sweet potatoes to bake in the brown sugar and pineapple juice.

We usually had our Easter meal around three. Everything was timed carefully around the ham and the Parker House rolls. About 30 minutes before H hour, my mother took the ham out of the oven and laid it out on a big sheet of wax paper, right in the middle of the kitchen table, to let it cool a bit and set—the thick, sweet, brown molasses and sugar oozing down over the sides, the pineapple slices baked brown, the cloves like tiny black insects soaking in the hot ham gravy.

Easter that year was the way all Easters should be but rarely are. Spring had come early, for a change. There were years when winter's hard rock ice was still visible along the curbs, blackened and filthy, coated with steel-mill grime, until late in May. But this Easter was different; gentle breezes blew through the kitchen screen door. Already the stickers in our yard gave promise of a bumper crop. The air was balmy and heavy with spring passion about to burst.

The spring sunlight slanted in through the kitchen window and bathed the ham in a golden, suffused light, just like any good religious experience should be lit. The old man was in an exalted state of anticipation. Whenever he really got excited, he would crack his knuckles loudly. On this fateful day, he was popping them like a set of Brazilian castanets. He had on the new white shirt that he had gotten the week before at J. C. Penney.

While the ham sat basking in our gaze, my mother busily spread the lace tablecloth on the dining-room table and set out our best china, which was used only three or four times a year at the maximum. My father picked up his carving knife again, for one last stroke on the whetstone. He held the blade up to the light. Everything was ready. He went into the living room and sat down.

"Ah."

His eyes glowed with the primal lust of a cave man about

to dig into the kill, which would last us at least four months. We would have ham sandwiches, ham salad, ham gravy, ham hash—and, finally, about ten gallons of pea soup made with the gigantic ham bone.

When it happened, he was sitting knee-deep in the *Chicago Tribune* sports section. I had been called in to wash up. My mother was in the bedroom, removing the curlers from her hair. My Aunt Glenn and Uncle Tom were on their way over to have Easter dinner with us. Uncle Tom always gave me a dollar. It was going to be a day to remember. Little did I suspect why.

I had just left the bathroom and my kid brother had just gone in for his fumigation, when suddenly and without warning:

BLAM!

The kitchen door flew open. It had been left ajar just a crack to let the air come in to cool the ham.

I rushed to the kitchen just in time to see 4293 blue-ticked Bumpus hounds roar through the screen door in a great, roiling mob. The leader of the pack—the one that almost got the old man every day—leaped high onto the table and grabbed the butt end of the ham in his enormous slavering jaws.

The rest of the hounds—squealing, yapping, panting, rolling over one another in a frenzy of madness—pounded out the kitchen door after Big Red, trailing brown sugar and pineapple slices behind him. They were in and out in less than five seconds. The screen door hung on one hinge, its screen ripped and torn and dripping with gravy. Out they went. Pow, just like that.

"HOLY CHRIST!" The old man leaped out of his chair. "THE HAM! THE HAM! THOSE GODDAMN DOGS! THE HAM!!"

He fell heavily over the footrest as he struggled to get into the kitchen, his voice a high-pitched scream of disbelief and rage. My mother just stood in the dining room, her face blank and staring, two aluminum hair curlers still in place. I ran through the kitchen, following my old man out to the back porch.

The snarling mob had rolled across the back yard and was now battling it out next to the garage, yipping and squealing with excitement. Occasionally, one of them would be hurled out of the pack, flipping over backward in the air, to land heavily amid the barrel staves and sardine cans. Instantly, he would be back in the fray, biting and tearing at whatever moved.

The ham didn't last eight seconds. Old Grandpa Bumpus and a dozen other Bumpuses stuck their heads out of various windows, to see what all the yowling was about. Without pausing to aim, he reared back and spit a great big gob of tobacco juice—a new long-distance record—right into the middle of the pack. It was a direct hit on our ham—or what was left of it.

He whooped wildly, wattles reddening with joy, spraying tobacco juice in all directions, while Cletus, his dimwitted grandson, yelled from the basement door:

"GAHDAMN, GRAN'PAW, LOOKA THEM HOUN'S GO! LOOKA THEM OL' BOYS GO! HOT DAMN!!"

Delbert, meanwhile, circled around the roaring inferno, urging them on, kicking dogs that had given up back into the fray. Suddenly, he looked up at where I was hiding, a sadistic grin on his face, his hair hanging low. Our eyes met significantly for a fleeting instant and then he went back to kicking. A paralyzing fear gripped me. I remembered! That time I threw him out at first! Was this what he meant? Was *I* responsible for this tragedy? Oh, God, no! I slunk back into the shadows.

Bumpus women, their lank hair streaming down over their red necks, cackled fiendishly. Emil Bumpus, who had been asleep under the front porch, came reeling out, trailing his jug of white lightning. He took one look and practically passed out, wheezing and harrumphing and gurgling with hilarity.

My old man just stood stock-still on the back porch for a long moment, and then he blew his stack. I had never seen him do anything before that came near what he did now. We kept bottles on the back porch to be returned to the grocery store. He reached down and grabbed a milk bottle. His face white with rage, he wound up mightily and, with a sweeping, sidearm motion, hurled the bottle against the side of the Bumpus house with a deafening crash.

Grandpa Bumpus stopped in mid-spit, a big juicy gob hanging down over his chin. Emil dropped his jug to the ground, eyes lighting up with joy. This was back home for

Emil. He was in his element. Turning around as if to run for his shotgun, he paused when he saw the old man standing there unmoving—radiating the clearest and most beautiful rage I'd ever seen in my life.

I cowered next to the railing on the back porch. Even the dogs felt his hatred. One by one, they fell silent. The bare, shiny bone of the ham lay in the sun. Big Red licked his chops.

After a long, pregnant moment, the old man turned, walked back into the kitchen and slammed the door. He stood for a minute by the kitchen table, looking down at the big sheet of wax paper dripping warm ham gravy. The heavenly aroma still hung heavy in the house. The old man just stood there—and came as close to crying as I'd ever seen him come.

Finally, he spoke, in a low, rasping voice: "All right! OK! Get your coats. We're going to the Chinese joint. We're going to have chop suey."

Ordinarily, this would have been a gala of the highest order, going to the chop-suey joint. Today, it had all the gaiety of a funeral procession. The meal was eaten completely in silence.

That was the beginning of the bitter Shepherd-Bumpus feud. Relentlessly, the old man beleaguered the Bumpuses at every moment. He had tap-dancing cleats put on his shoes, which proved to be quite a nasty surprise to Big Red the first day he tried his usual ankle grab and caught a cleat behind his left ear. The old man took up tobacco chewing and arched long, undulating gobs onto the Bumpuses front porch when the wind was right. Every time the Bumpuses cranked up for a Gene Autry record festival, the old man countered with *In a Persian Market* played at full blast on our Sears, Roebuck Silvertone phonograph.

He took to throwing beer bottles out of the kitchen window and hurling coffee grounds onto the roof of the Bumpus truck when it bellowed by, taking the Bumpuses down to pick up their weekly relief check. He put bottle caps and tacks in the driveway and laughed uproariously every time one of the Bumpus women fell out the back door. He planted stickers in the cave that the Bumpus hounds lived in under the garage and took to jumping up and down on the garage floor late at night, when the hounds were asleep. Once he even bayed at the moon louder than all the hounds put together. I still remember the startled look on Big Red's face when the old man let out a long, drawn-out, quavering howl that he had learned from 20 years of watching Tarzan pictures.

The only trouble was that nothing he did—but *nothing*—made the slightest dent on the Bumpus way of life. They didn't even seem to know he was doing anything. The bottle caps and tacks he threw in the driveway never even scratched their feet, horny-hard after generations of shoelessness. The only thing that came of it was that we got two flats in one day on the Olds. His pitiful tobacco juice added as much to the sea that the Bumpuses themselves produced as a raindrop in the ocean. Nothing he could do had any effect. One night, he told my mother he had concluded that the Bumpuses *planned* the ham raid, the dogs carrying out their orders like guerrilla fighters. He hinted that he had something up his sleeve that he was working out in the basement that would really settle the score once and for all. He was biding his time.

The Bumpuses, meanwhile, went on with life as usual. There wasn't much they could do to us that they hadn't already done without intending to. Grandpa Bumpus jacked up his output of tobacco juice a little, but the rest of them just went about their business—collecting junk and piling it in the yard, tossing potato peels out the window, brewing moonshine, hollering, hitting each other and scratching themselves.

Then one night, without warning, everything changed forever. I awoke suddenly about three A.M. with a strange feeling that something was wrong. It was. For a couple of minutes, I couldn't focus my mind; then, gradually, it became clear to me that something was up. I heard my father in the next room. He had apparently awakened about the time I had.

He said hoarsely to my mother, "Hey, wake up!"

Then a long period of silence, while he listened in the darkness. We were always having alarums and excursions, but this was really different.

The bedsprings squeaked and the old man's feet pattered across the bedroom floor; the usual thump and groan of excruciating pain as he stubbed the foot of the dresser. A rustling silence as he peered through the curtains into the blackness of the night.

"Shhhhh!"

Another pause. I waited, scared and anxious in my bed, my kid brother mewing softly across the room.

"I'll be damned!" the old man said aloud in wonder. "You'll never believe it."

"Believe what?" whispered my mother, who had gotten up and joined him.

"Just take a look out there," he said with disbelief. "They moved out! They're gone!"

I realized why I had awakened. For the first time in many months, the sound of Gene Autry records had ceased; the continuous whine and yelp of the Bumpus hounds had been silenced. Everything was—*quiet*.

My father sniffed noisily.

"The smell is gone. Even the smell is gone!"

It was true. The air in my bedroom was clear of cabbage, dog urine and corn whiskey for the first time in six months.

The next morning, the truth was there for all to see. The Bumpuses had packed up and moved on, leaving behind a sagging shambles of a house, the back yard rutted and ground to gray dust by the endless clawings and scratchings of the Bumpus dogs and the Bumpus chickens, with great, tangled rat's nests of rusting junk and weather-beaten barrels, and smelly gallon jugs and empty bean cans that told everything there was to know about the way the Bumpuses lived out their days. They just ran up a big enough rent bill and then moved out in the middle of the night. We never heard another word about them.

At first, my father seemed to be glad. Then, about a

month later, a nice old couple moved in next door and soon had the house and yard looking like an illustration for an insurance company that sold retirement plans to nice old couples. They went to bed every night at 8:30 and had a canary as a pet.

One night at supper, after a couple of beers, the old man finally said it:

"You know, they cleaned out just when I was going to hand 'em my crusher. I'll bet they did it on purpose." He got kind of moody for a while after that. We never found out what he had planned.

ABOUT THE AUTHOR

For many years a cult radio and cabaret personality in New York City, JEAN SHEPHERD was the creator of the popular film *A Christmas Story*, which is based on this book and has become a holiday tradition on the Turner Network. He was also the author of *A Fistful of Fig Newtons* and *The Ferrari in the Bedroom*, as well as *In God We Trust, All Others Pay Cash* and *Wanda Hickey's Night of Golden Memories*, both of which are available in Broadway paperback. Jean Shepherd passed away in 1999.